'95
Op

5=
LD-95

UNLESS SOUL CLAP ITS HANDS

Schocken Books
New York

Unless Soul Clap Its Hands

*Portraits
and Passages*

ERIKA DUNCAN

First American edition published by Schocken Books 1984
10 9 8 7 6 5 4 3 2 1   84 85 86 87

Library of Congress Cataloging in Publication Data
Duncan, Erika.
    Unless soul clap its hands.
    1. Duncan, Erika—Friends and associates.   2. Authors,
American—20th century—Biography.   3. Authors, English—
20th century—Biography.   4. American literature—20th
century—History and criticism—Addresses, essays, lectures.   5. English
literature—20th century—History and criticism—
Addresses, essays, lectures.   I. Title.
PS3554.U4636U5   1984   810'.9'0054 [B]   84–10641

Designed by Michael Starkman
Manufactured in the United States of America
ISBN 0–8052–3916–2

Acknowledgments for all copyright material used are given on pages 207–208,
which constitute an extension of this copyright page.

For my father,
Jacob Volkman,
And for my daughters,
Rachel, Gwynne, and Jane

CONTENTS

ACKNOWLEDGMENTS

First and mostly, I would like to thank Marshall Hayes of *Book Forum* for seeing in my earliest nonfiction the emergence of this portrait form, and for consistently publishing the finished pieces, one by one, as I produced them. Marilyn Wood, also of *Book Forum,* has offered her thoughtful readings and friendship over the years. For the existence of the English portraits, I thank Tracy O'Kates, who, hearing about my portrait work, brought me to London and offered me living space in her house in Hampstead. At Schocken Books, I would like to thank in particular my editor, Betty Gold, and Irene Williams for their consistent, warm support. I also extend my appreciation to all of the women who have passed through the Woman's Salon and through my fiction workshops, and to my undergraduate students of writing at New York University. Without their generous sharing of their experiences with the writing process at its earliest stage perhaps my questions would have been less profound. And finally I wish to thank my dear friends Karen Malpede, Leslie Tanner, and Ellen Marshall Reifler for the steadiness of their support throughout.

INTRODUCTION

"Now I believe in tellin, while we're live and goin roun. . . . There's a time ta tell and a time ta set still ta let a ghost grieve ya. . . . There's a time for live things and a time for dead, for ghosts and for flesh 'n bones: all life is just a sharin of ghosts and flesh. Us humans are part ghost and part flesh—part fire and part ash—but I think maybe the ghost part is the longest lastin," William Goyen wrote in *Ghost and Flesh, Water and Dirt,* in what was to become his own funeral oration. At the end of the summer of 1983, as I was beginning to collect my "Portraits of Living Writers" for this publication, William Goyen died.

I went to William Goyen's funeral with Marguerite Young. She told me that she had packed two china dolls' heads needing eyes and bodies, arms and legs. Would I come with her after the funeral to the New York Doll Hospital nearby? After every writer's funeral at Campbell's Funeral Home she always has a doll reassembled, she explained. It is her personal act of resurrection, continuity.

So too, I see each of these portraits as an act of reassembly, out of fragments, out of short, intensive meetings and long, solitary hours spread over the months and years reading each writer's full body of work. Written and originally published between 1977 and 1982, over a five-year period, the portraits are my attempt to catch the undercurrent of an era no longer so clearly seen, to bring to the surface some of the voices of this century which even at the present moment move toward places we imagine but cannot yet concretize in literary history.

The portraits are also my way of asking certain questions about the nature of the intersection of art and life, my way of

watching through the eyes and works of others who have
triumphed the vulnerable transmutation of early imprints
and later experiences into new essences larger than the self,
the transmutation of various kinds of caring, thinking, and
involvement, into story, into song.

Thus I have traveled to the Isle of Wight to listen to the
nearly three-decades long silence of David Gascoyne, child
prodigy who had written five books by the time he was
twenty and was known in England, France, and Spain. For
three full days I did not try to break the impact of his silence
while I sat with him reading his poems of prophecy, written
decades in the distance. I did not try to bring him back out of
that distance.

I have walked along Bleecker Street year after year, listening to Marguerite Young, author of the epic *Miss Macintosh, My Darling,* talk of the poetic symbolism of each new
detail that she was adding to her new epic biography of
Eugene Victor Debs. I've heard her interweave the facts and
tales of labor history she would unearth each day so lovingly
they all would turn to poetry, to myth.

Long nights, over the telephone, when it was cheap
enough to talk, Tillie Olsen told me stories about Ding
Ling, Tolstoy, and Gorki to make sure I understood the
meaning of her own involvement in the struggle of the
people. And lying on a sofa with her feet propped up, in the
home of the entertainment editor of the *Daily World,* Meridel
Le Sueur, born with the century, "the bloodiest century in
history, born with [her] hand in fist" and blacklisted for more
than thirty years, discussed her new attempt to write a novel
without any nouns because the nature of an object varies
according to the kindness or the cruelty of its situation and
its use.

Reading the hidden meanings of my every gesture as we
spoke, Charlotte Wolff told me of how once she studied the
hands of Antonin Artaud, André Breton, Virginia Woolf, and

Lady Ottoline Morrell. She told me of how she went from writing about the human hand, to gesture, and then finally to the study of human sexuality.

I talked with William Goyen about how he wanted his publisher to print his little *Book of Jesus,* written during a time of darkness and despair, to sell for fifty cents so that it could be given away on street corners or left on benches in deserted railway stations. I talked with Stanley Kunitz and Olga Broumas together at Yale University on the occasion of Olga Broumas's receipt of the Yale Younger Poets Prize. I asked Stanley Kunitz how he felt about giving the prize to a lesbian separatist and he replied, "If you stop being vulnerable, you die."

In a serene ground floor apartment in Paultons Square, between South Kensington and Chelsea, surrounded by her books and engravings from Blake and Milton, I talked to Kathleen Raine who told me that most of the poets she would send me to were dead, that the living person with whom she had best communicated was the tribal chieftain of the Hopis, because like herself he made no distinction between words and the things they were meant to represent.

I read and loved each writer and each work.

I have also included in this volume two portraits of writers I never met. Djuna Barnes, very much a presence here on Patchin Place, did not want to be met. I did not try to violate her wish while she was living still, nor later try to probe the secrets of her history. And yet I feel that without a short elegy to her and to her *Nightwood* this volume would not be complete. Mary Webb, alas, was not alive during my lifetime, and yet I feel that my discovery of her *Precious Bane* for years had the aura about it of a secret meeting. It was only after I published the "rediscovery" of her included here that I learned that others also had this feeling.

I had ended my rediscovery with a quotation from Mary Webb's handwritten "Poetry of the Prayer Book." Praying, she had written, was like "launching a wireless message in space. . . . Where it will go [we] cannot guess. Who will pick it up, how many will hear it, who will reply to it, how long it will go echoing away and away into the dark—all this is unknown. But does [the] message fail to be heard on that account? Surely not! Whoever is waiting for it will get it!"

"And so," I had written in *Book Forum*, "I feel about Mary Webb's writing itself, which came to me as such a message that perhaps I can pass on, those dear dust-covered volumes lost in long obscurity." Shortly after I published my article, James Langford, the director of the University of Notre Dame Press, discovered it and did bring out the first recent American reprint of *Precious Bane*.

And so I feel, not only about Mary Webb and *Precious Bane*, but about all of the works and writers in this volume. There is no underlying logic in the particular combination of writers presented here. One cannot categorize them, nor categorize their relationships to one another. Yet, each in her or his own way has moved me deeply, personally and artistically. It is my hope the readers "fishing here," as the wonderful blue sign above the old Gotham Book Mart says, may find a hidden pearl or two, that, out of the many messages, each reader may be reached by a writer or two, perhaps previously unknown, whose words will strike a chord, a wish for more. These portraits are my wireless messages, my pearls.

PORTRAITS

MARGUERITE YOUNG

ften I would meet Marguerite Young strolling down Bleecker Street with a quiet dignity, her woven Grecian bag draped diagonally over her many painted ponchos, walking beneath long and luxuriously embroidered Indian skirts, talking excitedly about her new biography of Eugene Victor Debs, stopping now and then to admire an angel in a store window, or an antique doll's head, or I would sit next to her on a yellow turning stool at Riker's Corner Restaurant, at the odd diagonal lunch counter, to listen to her talk of the crumbling of utopian quests in American life, the Don Quixote searches, and the Rappites and the Shakers and the Oneidas. Listening to her wonderful litanies about the Brisbanites, the Mormons, and the Marxist Buddhists, the millennial dreamers of the American Zion and the birds and beasts of socialism, looking at the gathered local Greenwich Village people, I would think rather nostalgically of the days when she had met with James Coco, the clown, and Mari Sandoz, chronicler of the vanishing American West, days

when Sheridan Square was the gathering place for a whole
creative community, now gone.

Most days she would wake up very early and begin to
write. She did not like to make appointments because they
would distract her from the inner rhythm of her writing,
which had become her drug and only love. From about
four-thirty in the morning until five at night she wrote, at
which hour she could almost feel her creative energy depart,
although she never checked the clock. Then she would walk
to Sheridan Square, to Riker's, to have coffee. Old friends
and followers would seek her out there to listen to her enchanted recounting of the stories from the daily newspapers
which would be spread out before her on the counter, stories
in which all things familiar and mundane were transformed
into vast poetic ballads, stories through which one heard
right away her love of the word and through which one
could catch a glimpse of the interior imagery and intricate
workings of her mind that made her kind of writing possible.
Although Marguerite Young loved to talk, she never stayed
out long.

Usually I would leave her at the doorway of the house
where Herman Melville once was said to have lived. I would
watch her slowly climb the stairs, imagining her making her
way through the crowd of China dolls, Charlie Chaplin
among them, arranged on broken velvet sofas and painted
Mexican chairs, going past the antique merry-go-round
horse that guards her door. Then I would think of her seated
at her desk surrounded by her ever-increasing collection of
books that far outnumber the bookshelves all along the
walls, among the saints and sea shells and the angel heads
and icons that abound in her red-walled apartment. And I
would feel a surge of youthful joy at knowing such a person.

I first met Marguerite Young when I was a student of
fiction writing in her class at the New School for Social
Research. I was attracted by her reputation as a teacher of

creative writing. More than two hundred of her students had published. Some had become quite well known. Indirectly she had been Flannery O'Connor's teacher. Flannery, whom she remembers as an absolutely silent, shy young girl, had been the student of one of her students.

Occurring in an age of stark rationalism and spare prose, Marguerite Young's teaching was particularly unique, as she conveyed not only a reverence for poetic language and fully rendered imagery, but also gave her students the courage "to carry their obsessions to their ultimate conclusions." *Miss Macintosh, My Darling,* her epic novel, which came out in 1965, became a kind of Bible for us, for in it we found an epic elegy for all creation, a poetic ode to man's futile search for perfection through which all of the beauties of the flawed soul in its striving were revealed. It was one of the few fully integrated syntheses of recent psychological discoveries and archetypal mythologies in our contemporary literature. Although I had grown up surrounded by psychologists, deeply immersed in psychoanalytic thinking, through Marguerite Young's imagistic unearthing of the multiple layers of illusions, obsessions, and memories which underlie all conscious thought, I found an understanding of the inner life far more profound than any I had ever known. Every time I picked up her book I felt that I embarked upon a tidal voyage through great oceans of psychic time and space. Enveloped by a multitude of calling choral voices, male and female, dead and living, ancient, mythical, and modern, imaginary and real, I found myself drawn by Marguerite Young's recurrent sublingual rhythms into emotional realms which transcended all rational thought.

As a teacher, and later as a kind of mentor, Marguerite Young emitted a vision of largeness and plurality, of perpetual pregnancy with the dream. (One of my favorite characters in *Miss Macintosh, My Darling* is Esther Longtree, who is perpetually pregnant with the shadow child, the imaginary baby who embodies all her hopes, her history, and dreams.) Marguerite Young never limited her teaching to the techniques of writing, but rather shared her own enthusiasm about the multiplicity of fields of learning and life understanding from which great literature is made. Her lectures combined discourses upon philosophy, psychology, and religion with news stories and personal ancedotes in ways which shed amazing light upon the connection between the small details and tangible traces of our human lives, our little idiosyncracies, and their more cosmic meanings. Her lectures would alert us to the hidden logic in the most contradictory aspects of human nature, the inherent order in the chaos, if only we would dare let down our guard and enter it.

Often she used to quote Freud, who said that the only difference between a genius and a mediocre writer was that the genius had no toll-keeper at the gate. She talked frequently of "beautiful horse-faced George Eliot," of Henry James and Proust and Melville, and of other writers she had loved. She would tell us about how three-year-old Edgar Allan Poe had been in bed with his young actress mother for several hours after she died, explaining how that period of waiting for her eyes to open had led to the eternal confusion of death and living in Poe's work, his quest for resurrection. I could never hear enough of these stories.

Or she would lecture about *The Compulsion to Confess* according to Theodore Reik, William James's *Variety of Religious Experience,* or Bishop Berkeley's theory of solipsism in which the whole of reality would perish with the closing of the eye. But always interwoven with these theoretical lectures would be the simplest stories of the people whom we saw or read of daily: Patty Hearst, Spiro Agnew's little daughter, Jimmy Carter who intrigues her because he wraps his peanuts up in Xerox copies of his favorite Dylan Thomas poems, and the local man in rags who wears a tin-foil crown, who really is a multimillionaire but has forgotten.

When Marguerite Young was a child, her maternal grandmother who raised her used to read to her the Bible and Grimm's fairy tales. By the age of twelve she knew the Bible intimately and was beginning to do a great deal of thinking in French. She fell madly in love with Anatole France, with Balzac, Racine, and Voltaire. Possessing a natural linguistic gift coupled with an obsession for all things French, she took seriously a French teacher's statement that "If it was not beautiful it was not French" and early began to develop a beauty in her own language. Her grandmother used to take her upon her knee, holding a little pencil in her hand, and tell her that either she would be a great writer or the first woman president of the United States.

Her grandmother was a very literary and artistic person who wanted her to be everything she herself might have been if women of her time had been more free. When the young Marguerite was "writing her first book," her papers spread over the living room rug "like a red sea" through which only her grandmother and she could find the path, her grandmother used to send all visitors around to the side door so that the child's efforts would not be disturbed. Even now, the floors of her apartment are spread with a similar sea of manuscripts, so thick that it is hard to walk, the piles of papers intermingled with opened old grey-purple tomes from second-hand bookstores and new dollar remaindered books from Marboro with glossy-paper jackets lettered in bold type.

Violently opposed to the anti-intellectual current in the modern literary world, Marguerite Young is a lover of all learning. "Knowledge is power," she says, "if it is synthesized with emotion." Herself a scholar in fields as far divergent as criminology, ornithology, and religion, she feels that literature is but one arc in a great circle of knowledge, that only through real familiarity with the other arcs in the circle can vision widen and imagery be transformed from ornament to symbol. The other day, while exclaiming upon the merits of higher education, she remarked drolly, "I doubt that out of our own consciousness would ever come the fact that sea urchins steer by the north star, or that the Indians believed that owls have lights in them by which to navigate at night."

She often expresses her gratitude to the many important scholars who have taught her: Baskerville, Ronald Salmon Crane (who made her read *Tom Jones* thirteen times), and Robert Morse Lovett, the Milton scholar who believed that God was Charles Stuart and the devil was Oliver Cromwell. While she was studying the emblems and symbols of seventeenth-century and Elizabethan literature at the University of Chicago, completing her thesis on the birds and beasts of Euphues's England, she took a job reading Shakespeare aloud to an "opium lady," a patroness of the arts and close friend of Thornton Wilder, who often used to come and stay all night to talk. There she slept in the bed where Edna St. Vincent Millay had slept (something which was much more important to her then than it would be now, she says), or else roller-skated home along the lake shore through the darkened city. There she was offered opium every day, which she always refused, earning her the nickname of "the prosaic sprite." She was present during many of the opium lady's dreams and overheard her dialogues with long dead visitors. She was there when the golden cockerel perched on the opium lady's bedpost and when the life-sized blackbird came up to her door. Doctors and psychologists would be running through the house reading Elizabeth Barrett Browning and De Quincy, trying to understand opium addiction, and the whole Jewish intellectual circle of Hyde Park, at that time second only to Vienna's, would converge there. Years later when she be-

gan to write her epic novel, the opium lady became one of
the central characters, as a way of exploring the unconscious as well as the interplay of reality and illusion.

At around this time she spent two weeks with Gertrude
Stein and Alice B. Toklas in a special seminar with Thornton
Wilder. She remembers how Gertrude Stein would wear a
garnet when she was formally dressed and remove it when
she was not. She remembers how Gertrude Stein would
stand before the class in all her grandeur proclaiming, "I've
earned my eccentricities!" and how she would go around in a
police van on rainy nights "looking for crimes" and never
finding them.

For a while Marguerite Young lived in Shelbyville,
Kentucky, the home of Colonel Shelby of *Uncle Tom's Cabin.*
There she wrote poetry in the graveyards, as she was later to
do in the beautiful little Wabash River town of New Harmony, the scene of two Utopias, where her mother and step-
father owned the motion picture business. "I do think the
pleasures of being a graveyard poetess are very great," she
said to me, "especially if there are lovely epitaphs upon the
tombstones, and crumbling angel wings. I spent endless
summers in New Harmony watching the quail rustling
through the old Rappite graveyard where there were no
tombstones, the Rappites having wished not to have the task
of rolling away the tombstones when the angel Gabriel blew
his river horn."

Marguerite Young was a poet from the age of seventeen
until the age of twenty-four. She published two books of
poems, *Prismatic Ground* and *Moderate Fable,* which was the
winner of the American Academy of Arts and Letters Award.
She became close to the poets of the Southern Fugitive
Group, Allen Tate, John Crowe Ransom, and Robert Low-
ell, who wanted to adopt her because they thought that she
was really a Southerner who had the misfortune to be born
above the Mason-Dixon Line. And indeed it is her "South-

ern" love of the tale which caused her to transform her native Indiana into the legendary landscape that Anaïs Nin termed "the nocturnal America," the very opposite of the bland, flat picture of the Middle West so many people seem to have. Once when Marguerite Young was at the Algonquin Bar she was accosted by a red-faced man who introduced himself as Sinclair Lewis. Tired of imitators, he expressed his pleasure at seeing a totally different view of his part of the country.

Through her poetry, Marguerite Young got to know Harriet Monroe, the editor of *Poetry: A Magazine of Verse*. She would often visit her in her Chicago apartment on East Erie Street, with its windowsills lined with beautiful Chinese dolls, where all the poets came. There, she recalls, you would feel that you were in the presence of Carl Sandburg, Vachel Lindsay, Edgar Lee Masters, Peter De Vries, and the many others who had passed through. Marguerite Young received a letter from Harriet Monroe, written the day before she died climbing the Andes Mountains that she always wrote about.

Although Marguerite Young abandoned poetry as a separate form shortly after the publication of *Moderate Fable,* her poetry never really stopped but rather grew to become a strong and central aspect of her prose, her earlier images and poetic preoccupations constantly reappearing, and expanding in symphonic swells throughout her later work. *Angel in The Forest,* her first major work of prose, an epic tale of the two Utopias that had flourished in New Harmony whose history she came to know while living there, was the beginning of her inquest into illusion. She confessed to me, "I would never have been drawn to write about Robert Owen and the history of the British labor movement, if Owen had not started out his career with a debate with Coleridge as to whether or not there were unearthly spirits in the deep. Owen said there were not, that life was rational and man was a machine, but when he was old and deaf he saw and conversed with many spirits in the deep, among them Coleridge, Shelley, the Duke of Kent, and Benjamin Franklin."

After Marguerite Young left Chicago she went for a while to Shortridge, a suburb of Indianapolis, where she taught both retarded and genius children. She enjoyed both groups and was grateful to be spared teaching the average, whom she feels are much less open to imagery and symbolic interpretations than either of the extremes, for both extremes respond to metaphor, although only the genius might retain its meaning. It was at this school that she first met Kurt Vonnegut, then a student there, who has remained a lifelong friend. Later she went on to do advanced graduate work at the University of Iowa. While reading case histories by the ton, she became very involved in the psychology of William James. One winter when she was snowbound in "the Arctic Wasteland of Iowa City," she read the entire work of Madame Blavatsky, the theosophist mystic, who was a great influence upon Yeats, whom she used as a model for the opium lady in *Miss Macintosh, My Darling*.

Marguerite Young had had many dreams that she could never realize because she came of age during the depression years. One of the first poems she ever wrote begins. "Wait for me, Oh wait for me/Towns of France and Germany/I am coming by and by . . . ," but it was many years before she got to Europe. Very few people could afford to do things like that in those days. She had also dreamed of riding through the Kentucky mountains on mule back collecting ballads, but she did not have the fifty dollars for the mule.

When Marguerite Young first came to New York City, Edna St. Vincent Millay was still alive and could be seen sometimes at Number One Fifth Avenue, Kathleen Millay could be seen drinking at Chumley's and Nora Millay ran a lampshade shop in the neighborhood nearby. Often she would see e.e. cummings crossing Washington Square, or catch a glimpse of Djuna Barnes who appeared at one of

Allen Tate's parties wearing a chinchilla muff in June. She
also knew Louise Bogan, famous for her *New Yorker* book
review of William Faulkner's first novel which made the
dire prediction, "Here is another young man from whom not
much can be expected."

With Leo Lerman, Marguerite Young went to many
beautiful parties, among them Maya Deren's fantastic evenings. For a Princeton party, she lent Allen Tate a Spanish
army officer's cape, a bust of Pallas, and a raven so that he
could go disguised as Poe. And now, on a sundial table in
the middle of her apartment, there sits a stuffed black crow
named Edgar Allan Tate Poe. She spoke lovingly of Owen
Dodson who dedicated to her a book about black preachers
in the South, and of Ray West who claimed he wrote his
book on Brigham Young because he got tired of all of Marguerite Young's questions about her ancestor. The book
took him nine years to write.

For a year she had watched a woman madly writing with
a red pencil in the Village Drug Store, telling herself that no
real writer would try to work that way, when she found out
that the woman was Mari Sandoz, the Indian historian whose
poetic tales of Buffalo Bill and others she had long admired.
Mari Sandoz had sought the noisiest place she knew in order
to do the final editing of her work, the multiple distractions
preventing her from censoring herself too rigorously. Mari
Sandoz, who on her deathbed wrote the last pages of her
book on Custer's last stand, became one of her closest
friends. Marguerite Young introduced her to Anaïs Nin.
Now they are both gone. "They were older than I," she
mused, "but I feel very much like Oliver Wendell Holmes,
like the last leaf on the bough. These older writers were like
lighthouses for me. It was a great aristocratic cousinry with
very deep roots."

When Marguerite Young's editor, Frank Taylor, first introduced her to George Davis at Longchamps, George Da-

vis asked "Where is she?" and insisted that she was too young to be the author of *Angel in the Forest.* "The author of *Angel in the Forest* is someone who has spent her entire lifetime writing one book," he said. It turned out to be a prophetic statement.

Marguerite Young had not planned to write a novel. One day, Frank Taylor, her editor, invited her to his Connecticut home to spend a weekend. They missed the train and had a drink at Grand Central Station. They missed the second train and had a second drink. As she was not in the habit of drinking much, she remembers nothing further until the following morning when she woke up in Connecticut with a large check in her purse and a contract for a novel. Being poor at the time, she decided to set her book in an elegant New England house full of magnificent antiques and many echoes, ghosts, and dreams. This giant tapestry of tales composed of many minute threads of meaning drawn from many layers of the mind, populated with the most interesting people she had known or read of remolded into larger-than-life composites of mythic dimensions, all living out a multiplicity of strange obsessions, became the work of eighteen years. When at last it was completed, Frances Steloff, founder of the legendary Gotham Book Mart, hung a huge sign across her store window joyously proclaiming, "Marguerite Young has finished her book," and James Joyce's younger sister May greeted Marguerite Young with a warm embrace, congratulating her upon just having missed her brother's record in the writing of *Ulysses* by six months.

When *Miss Macintosh, My Darling* was published in England, Marguerite Young was given the choice of visiting any place she wished. Not surprisingly she chose to visit Scotland Yard, where she was shown the scenes of all the famous crimes. She also visited the graves of all the writers that she loved. With the present curator of Shandy Hall, she went out to the vegetable patch where Laurence Sterne was temporarily buried and talked to him. With Howard Griffin, who was one of Auden's closest friends, she visited the graves of George Eliot and Karl Marx, whom she loves for "the poet in him." Now Howard Griffin and W.H. Auden too are gone. Marguerite Young spoke of how terribly saddened she was by Auden's death which she "took as a deep personal loss, because he was the star of [her] generation" and recalled how she had given him a bedspread once.

Those years when I was Marguerite Young's student seem far away now. Much has happened in my own life since then. But often, when in a wistful mood, I will walk down Bleecker Street and think about the many long midsummer evenings I spent strolling there with her, listening to her magically meandering tales, evenings during which the love for writing which has become the meaning of my life grew up in me. Or sometimes I will walk past the corner restaurant which used to be Riker's, now Chico's Taco Rico, thinking of the time, when in the throes of finishing my first novel, I had staggered there, crazed from the sense of loss that all completions bring, to ask her if she really meant what she had always said, that finishing a book was just like dying. "Of course," she had replied, somewhat bored. "How normal! It means that you are really finishing and don't just think you are. It is just like the great auk trying to lay its last egg before extinction, or like the trapeze artist taking his final leap before the cheering audience, and when you are making that leap, people should not throw tin cans at you." Then she had quickly changed the subject to the surreal happenings of the day.

One summer evening recently, I walked into Pennyfeathers, the restaurant across the square from Riker's which closed down, where all her followers now go. She and some students were sitting at one of the staid wooden tables, no longer perched uncomfortably on the swivel stools where I had spent so many hours, and a small circle of smiling waiters, local theater people, and friends had gathered around them to listen to a new song, written in her honor by Jim Rado, co-composer with Jerry Ragni, of the Broadway musical, *Hair,* a lively jingle entitled, *Oh My Gosh Miss Macintosh.* And listening, watching the faces all around lit by a loving reverence, I drew a deep breath, knowing that I had partaken in a very special magic.

WILLIAM GOYEN

William Goyen's short stories and novels, most of which are based upon his East Texas roots but written over many decades of wandering far from home, are rich with the bizarre and wildly tragic quality that we have come to associate with Southern fiction. Not unexpectedly we find the plethora of hopelessly entangled families in which no member can escape the inadvertent wounds caused by the onward life course of the others, the familiar abundance of itinerant evangelists wandering forever homeless in search of the holy energy that cannot be truly found, the multitude of deformed and mutilated people who are stared at and exploited, the cold metal shotguns hidden under pillows of the mad, and even the relentless white roosters crowing until disaster comes, the plagues, the flagpole sitters, and the immense biblical birds of doom. But as we read further and allow ourselves to be captivated by Goyen's recurring song-like sorrowful refrains, his very personal transformation of his local dialect to poetry, we realize that despite the expected images and icons, the similarity in the

situations and stories explored, William Goyen's work is
strangely lacking in the cruelty and violence common to
most other writing from the South. Although, like Flannery
O'Connor, he focuses upon redemption, his vision is much
gentler and he seems to substitute compassion and a loving
human healing for O'Connor's cleansing by intense hellfire
and clear sight of sin.

When I went to visit William Goyen, I asked him how it
was that he had seen the same wild and weird violence that
the other Southern writers saw, had heard the same irrational
and scathing tales, yet wrote of them without a trace of wrath
or of brutality. He told me that he did not know exactly why
that should be, only that he had always felt that he was there
to help, that if he could enter the pain of others personally,
he might be able to free them from it. When he was a child
this overriding sense of mission got him into a lot of trouble,
before he learned to channel it into his art. He was always
"bringing strange, odd people home." If there was a crippled
boy in his class, he would bring him home. His family had
so much pain, he was surrounded by it. In beginning to
write, he had felt that he was called upon to be their mes-
senger and tell it, otherwise they would never be heard.

Very often William Goyen's writing seems to speak on
an almost sublingual level, his words becoming vehicles for
something else more primitive in resonance, kin to folk music in stark simplicity of impact. His novels and even his
shorter tales do not conform to our standard notion of plot,
but rather are circular in form, the slow unfolding of the
stories arising in waves which swell from recurring thematic
refrains reminiscent of the choruses of ballads, the rhythmic
repetition of these often plaintive calls drawing the reader
ever backwards in time and memory, like undertow against
the forward motion of the tale.

He spoke to me of how he had started to write during the
war when he was stationed on a ship surrounded by death

and destruction. He had never known such darkness and despair, such fear. Then one night he had gone out upon the deck and called his family, naming the members one by one. The night was cold, and as he called he saw his breath turn into substance in the fog, becoming more visible with every name he spoke, until it seemed that his whole house of childhood and his past was contained in its aura. The "naming" became a salvation, a *real* action which helped him keep the memory of his personal meaning when all else seemed lost. For it was in the calling of those people's names that they existed and it was in that visionary moment of watching his own breath materialize in the cold twilight with his "telling" that William Goyen realized that "everything that happened seemed to be in the speaking of it." After that he had begun to write *The House of Breath,* the story of those people, one piece at a time, until it turned into a book, his first.

It is this intuitive grasp of the extraordinary within our ordinary experience, the cosmic within the simple, that is very characteristic of William Goyen and his work. In his New York study, jars of scissors, pens and pencils, rabbits feet and dime store medals, alternate with ponderous volumes of Dante and Genet. Two old-fashioned wrought iron school desks stand in the center of the room, bolted to each other. On one there is an electric typewriter connected by infinities of tangled wires to an outlet far away. On the other is an enormous unabridged dictionary. Piles of papers, odd manuscript pages, and letters from publishers are held in place by miniature glass and china farm animals, and ornate old-world draperies and wallpapers mix up their patterns with the homey prints of cotton-covered cushions of all shapes and sizes, thrown on all the sofas and the chairs. One cannot see the Upper West Side city street outside because of all the plants that fill the window and the scalloped brown-fringed curtains, but the sun comes in. On the walls

occasional family pictures hang with theater posters and
scrawled pencil love letters from children.

We were speaking of Edith Wharton, about whom I happened to be writing, when William Goyen turned to five
luminous purple bulbs behind him, set in a glass candy dish
filled up with stones. "I love Edith Wharton," he said, "because she was in the dark so very long, just like a bulb which
must be kept out of the light while it springs its deep underground roots, seeming to be a dry dead thing." Then he
began to describe the incredible beauty of the first shoot of
green, speaking of Easter and the time of resurrection, "our
hope and our life."

On a high shelf backed with ornate French wallpaper lies
a picture book about the Big Thicket, sandwiched in between Carl Jung's *Man and His Symbols* and *The Realms of
Arthur*. I commented upon the juxtaposition and William
Goyen laughed. It made perfect sense, he said. Actually, he
had read all three books simultaneously, for wasn't his native Big Thicket like King Arthur's forest, "an enchanted
wood and wilderness where deeds took place."

Then suddenly he was speaking of T.S. Eliot, "who sings
such a forlorn song about kings and palaces and gas works."
The poets he feels closest to are Eliot and Pound, "men of
immense learning who sing the simplest songs." A lover of
opera, "a telling in which stories are sung," he had wanted to
be a musician originally, but he was much too poor to study
music and his family thought it improper for a boy to pursue
such studies seriously. He saved up all the money he earned
working at the local commissary for a subscription to a
mail-order piano lesson series and received a cardboard key-
board upon which he composed the grandest songs. He also
managed to buy himself a Victrola and one record, "The
Unfinished Symphony," which he used to listen to in bed
each night, hidden under a big heavy quilt so no one else
could hear. It was only after it became apparent that he could

not become a composer that he "settled for words," knowing
that they were only "second best." At first he feared he
would not find enough words (his curiosity for books came
late, since he was not from a reading family) but later they
"just poured out."

The people he grew up among talked easily and told a lot.
There was a natural use of hyperbole in their language, an
enhancement of things, and an appreciation of the commonplace, a finding of the extraordinary in small things. As a
child he heard the simplest stories, yet the telling made them
something grand. He spoke of how Olympian vision must
grow organically, out of the ordinary life which one cannot
be false to, because, like nature, it is inviolable. That is why
he could never write a story on commission. But, if one
listens carefully, out of the commonplace the most amazing
revelations come.

"A Shape of Light," an early story in which Goyen retells
the local folk myths which grew up around the famous
"ghost light" in the thicket begins relatively simply: ". . . So
the record reads: 'If on an evening of good moon you will
see a lighted shape, much like a scrap of light rising like a
ghost from the ground, then saddle your horse and follow it
where it will go. . . . Some old timers here call this Bailey's
Light and say that it is the lantern of a risen ghost of an old
pioneer, Bailey was his name."

At first this seems to be merely a collage of legends
superimposed upon one another and made human in the
telling by Goyen's personal entry into them. However,
gradually as the fusion of the layered tales intensifies, we
realize that we are being asked to follow not just one man's
mad pursuit of an illusionary glowing made of light of moon
on dust motes, but the search of every human being for the
radiance of life and hidden meaning in the darkness. In his
slow and seemingly simple retelling of these superimposed
stories, William Goyen is taking us on a spiritual voyage in

the quest for God and for illumination, ever so gently, hardly telling us where he is taking us and why.

Well, then, let me see here how to tell it, for I tell you this man had seen a strange and most marvelous passing thing and now has made me see it; and to fasten it in a telling and hold it recorded that way, though it itself run on, is all my aim and craving, find I tongue to tell it. I will want to tell you how, after seeing this light rise up and glide, a man got up to leave whatever he was doing to follow; and how the following of this light came to be the one gesture of his life. . . .

What put the blessing of the light upon him that turned his flesh to fire, that turned his eyes away from everything that would keep them from the path of the light? What serpent urged him to this record to get for himself this knowledge and this image which changed him into something he could only be by himself, something which he wanted to give to others (what a mystery that what was his light became others' darkness) yet which seemed to destroy them or turn them away from him? Was the light, then, death? Was the light, then, his own image of himself, which, given to others, stole their own self-image from them and left them him-imagined, without even the light to go after? What to proclaim out of this man's gesture, light or darkness?

William Goyen, forever following the ghost light of his art into the realms of other's darknesses, is very conscious of his own separateness, of being part ghost and part flesh ("I would love to stay here but I can't. I must go on."). He knew early that he was alienated from the people who were closest to him, that because of what he was doing (his art had to be kept secret from them), he would one day have to leave to meet them. On his writing desk there is a luminous blue lamp base, William Goyen's light of childhood which he carried with him all over the world, trying to find some one who could make it work. Sometimes, even now, when he goes away for a weekend, he brings it with him. Once he even left it with a highly recommended repairman for three weeks, but nothing could restore it. On its bare socket with no bulb or shade lies a curled up white rosary with beads that seem to come from a baby's hospital bracelet, a gift from one of William Goyen's students. The rosary had belonged to the student's father and when he died the student had handed it to William Goyen, knowing that he could not speak.

The blue-glass lamp appears often as a momentary image in Goyen's fiction, now sheltered under a poor tent of gauze and chenille from a cosmic indoor rainstorm reminiscent of the original flood, now more far away and fleeting, as do the interweaving themes of resurrection and illumination. For it is the quest for light which becomes both the isolating factor of the artist's life, the force which brings the pain of knowing, and yet the whole meaning of existence.

Because he followed the light, lo here! lo there! time and time again, every time he saw it, he knew where the light went, he found its secret territory. Something was there for him to find out and he had to endure, wait, study and study until its buried, difficult meaning came to him. But it didn't finally come, when it came, like an easy vision. He had to *follow,* hard and in hardship and torment, he had to give himself wholly, unafraid, surrendered to it. He had to leave things behind. When he left the territory of his meaning, his burden was to bear, understanding the meaning at last, what he had found out, and was to pass it on—and this was his life, bearing, suffering the found-out meaning of what he was involved in, haunted by it, grieved by it, but possessing it—and watching it continue to grow, on and on, into deeper and larger meaning. This, only, was all his pain.

One of William Goyen's earliest stories, "Nests in a Stone Image," ends with the description of a man who lies "like a star, in a kind of new curious steadfastness, feeling himself calm purity, deep clarity, clear cold star . . ." William Goyen considers this stellar luminosity, this "coming out clear," one of the most vital functions of art. He believes that art is redemption, that salvation comes through clarifying and resolving other people's suffering and "coming out whole, in a way." For him, writing has eased the suffering of entering other people's pain, has given him a missionary sense of healing: "Let me take your pain because I will be able to use it and transmute it."

Several weeks after I interviewed William Goyen, as I was rereading his work, I became obsessed with the desire to locate his little *Book of Jesus,* briefly mentioned in an interview with Goyen in the *Paris Review.* I walked for miles and miles, telephoning the Gotham Book Mart and the Strand, Brentanos, Barnes and Noble, and even the Calvary Book Store on Fifty-seventh Street, but no one had heard of the book. Finally, in a state of near frenzy, I called William Goyen and told him that I needed to know his Jesus in order to write about him, that I needed to know his God.

A few hours later I found myself in the hospital with my eight-year-old daughter who had broken her nose. As she lay frightened in her steel-barred bed awaiting her operation, I took out William Goyen's short stories and started to read them aloud. The ward was filled with black and Puerto

Rican children whose mothers could not be there, and I was the only adult in the room. As I began to read, a black girl who had hardly moved since I was there sat up in bed to hear the story of Old Mrs. Woman, Sister Sammye, and Little Pigeon, three lonely old women who took turns being ghosts so that the haunted household that they formed would not have to feel empty. The black girl stuck her white bandaged hand taped up with intravenous feeding tubes through the bed bars in order to better support herself. She smiled a quiet smile and seemed to take each word I read into her being as a healing. At first I had been reading rather hesitantly and softly. After all, this was hardly a children's story, and I was in a very strange, sad place. But later I let my voice rise full of all of William Goyen's passion, following his cadence and his song, until I felt that his spirit, his Jesus and his God, filled up the room and healed us all. I tell this story here only because I so deeply believe that art must be able to provide us with spiritual nurturance, that true immersion in a work of art is the highest form of religious experience, and because I believe that William Goyen's work, written with all his being, penetrates the depths from which such religious response can come.

A week later I told William Goyen the story of how I had found his Jesus in the hospital room, and asked him how he happened to write *A Book of Jesus,* his intimate retelling of the tale of Christ. It was during a time of great personal despair that he became obsessed with rediscovering Jesus. He was frantic, like a maniac, seized by his obsession. He argued with his publishers who were not particularly interested in the idea and fought and fought with them until he persuaded them to sign a contract for the book he felt he had to write. It was around Easter time, he said, that time of dying and rebirth ("I really do die and come back!"). He had wanted them to put the little volume out for fifty cents, so that he could go hand it out on street corners or leave it on benches in railroad stations. He was very disappointed when they produced a quality hardcover version for four-fifty. Although he had rarely talked about his writing before, he found himself telling the story of Jesus at every literary cocktail party and event, following "that ancient compulsion to bring the news." Often people would think he was making the story up. He took great pleasure in accepting invitations from universities to read from "his new novel" and, without any forewarning of the nature of his tale, reading the entire *Book of Jesus* from cover to cover, receiving tremendous response.

William Goyen said to me that he believes all art is about the absence or presence of that power of love which he discovered in the writing of *A Book of Jesus. Come the Restorer,* the novel which immediately follows *A Book of Jesus,* is both a return to his older works, rich in the legends of East Texas and the local folktales, and a branching out into something slightly freer, more surreal, more mythic, and more whimsical. In place of much of the old pain and sorrow that only the telling of the tale could heal, we find a quality of hope, of sexual energy, and of regeneration. Although, like Goyen's earlier works, this book reverberates with plaintive cries for the lost past which cannot be, there is a constant quality of partial mending, of rebirth and human trying from which the redemption comes.

Nothing but death is unrepairable, said Mr. de Persia, the repairman. Can't raise Lazarus, but can make what's dead *look* like life. They 'restored' that painting in the City Hall, damaged by water . . . that ancient church that was destroyed by fire . . . but can human feelings be 'restored,' Mr. de Persia? *Never the same, but yes* . . . once it has been broken. In a state of permanent inner disrepair. Yes, there are all the pieces back in their place. But the life between the pieces is gone, the joining life, the unseen running current of vitality. . . . When something is repaired, it is the wholeness of it that is not there any longer in that thing: that is gone forever. The entirety of it, the one-ness of it is shaken and leans from its foundation, it's off its center. Its core is disturbed, from which forces extend, flow out and issue; from which its vitality—egg force—horns out and beaks out, breaks through crust, like a blind chick in an egg. How to repair the disturbed egg of something? Oh, Mr. de Persia, restorer, proud repairman, can you restore or mend anything of *that?*

For William Goyen, the act of writing, the telling of the tale, becomes a "keeping" in the most sacred sense, a way of retaining not only those ghosts of the actual past, but the spirit ghosts of the unrealized loves and longings that haunt us all. Throughout his work one hears the calling of vanished voices, both from the past which is irreparably gone and from the wished-for future which can never be. His writing is an act of restoration and retention in words of that which can never be truly restored or kept, yet stays with us in the deepest recesses of our souls, the lingering memory within which calls us from our life of doing and of flesh, towards the earlier echos we both fear and crave.

In this season of Easter, William Goyen's favorite season of regeneration and rebirth, I went to all the New York City bookstores looking for the works of this spiritual healer and I could not find them. I remembered how William Goyen had told me that for nearly five years he had stopped writing altogether, because he had felt that he did not have any listeners, because contemporary readers had turned away from spirituality in books. His mother-in-law had come to him during those years and had implored him to talk to her, to tell him his tales. "Forget that I am here," she had said. "I am only two ears and two hands upon a typewriter." At first she had written his words down for him. Then, gradually, he had begun to write again himself. She had told him to forget that she was there, but it was only because of her presence, because of the certainty of a listener in the dark that he was able to begin to work again, to emerge again out of what he was later to describe as a "death time," not only for himself but for many fine writers in America.

TILLIE OLSEN

*I*n Yonnondio, *Tillie Olsen's "novel of the thirties," there*
is a scene in which the mother takes her children to
the outskirts of town to look for dandelion greens to eat.
Demoralized by the family's constant movement in search of
a better life, from the mining town where the pits devour
living men, to the beautiful rolling farm where hope is
gradually devoured by slow starvation and the inability to
own any of the beauty (where baby chickens, rescued from
freezing in the snow, are put into the oven to warm a bit and
roasted to a burnt crisp because nobody in the family has the
leftover energy to nurture anything, no matter how little), to
the meat packing town—burdened, numbed by the coming
of each new baby, by the hardening of the older children
who are drifting and frightened and falling, the mother suddenly notices a loveliness in the patterns of the opening
leaves and blossoms. Only for a moment, she can hold her
oldest daughter Mazie in her arms and sing.

In deference to the original form of the portraits, I have kept the thirties
focus in my study of Tillie Olsen, first written for *Book Forum*'s "Thirties"
issue.

A remote, shining look was on her face . . . as if
she had become someone else, was not their mother
any more, "Ma, come back," Mazie felt like yelling, in
rancor, in fear; jumping up, snapping her fingers into
that dreaming face to bring attention, consciousness
of them back, make it the old known face again . . .

"My head is balloony, balloony," [the mother
says.] "Balloony." She staggered, put her arms
around Mazie, sang:

> O Shenandoah I love thy daughter
> I'll bring her safe through stormy water

smiled so radiantly, Mazie's heart leapt. Arm in arm,
they sat down under the catalpa. That look was on
her mother's face again, her eyes so shining and
remote. She began stroking Mazie's hair in a kind of
languor, swoon. Gently and absently she stroked.

> Around the springs of gray my wild root weaves,
> Traveler repose and dream among my leaves

her mother sang. A fragile old remembered comfort
streamed from the stroking fingers into Mazie,
gathered to some shy bliss that shone despairingly
over suppurating hurt and want and fear and sham-
ings—the Harm of years. River wind shimmered
and burnished the bright grasses, her mother's hand
stroked. stroked.

> I saw a ship a sailing
> A sailing on the sea

Mazie felt the strange happiness in her mother's
body, happiness that had nought to do with them,
with her; happiness and farness and selfness.

> I saw a ship a sailing
> And on that ship was me.

The fingers stroked, spun a web, cocooned
Mazie into happiness and intactness and selfness.
Soft wove the bliss round hurt and fear and want
and shame—the old worn fragile bliss, a new
frail selfless bliss, healing, transforming. Up from
the grasses, from the earth, from the broad tree
trunk at their back, latent life streamed and
seeded. The air and self shone boundless. Absently her mother stroked; stroked unfolding,
wingedness, boundlessness.

"I'm hungry," Ben said . . .

The wind shifted, blew packing house. A tremble
of complicity ran through Mazie's body; with both
hands she tethered her mother's hand to keep it
stroking. Too late. Something whirred, severed,
sank. *Between a breath, between a heartbeat, the weight
settled, the bounds reclaimed.*

Never again, but once, did Mazie see that look—
the other look—on her mother's face.

But flickering within that fleeting look is Tillie Olsen's
conviction that within each human being lies a potential that
no amount of oppression or suppression can completely kill,
a potential which makes both personal and political action
imperative. It is the faith in this potential lodged in the
human being alone (and not in "larger" incomprehensible
forces) which moves Tillie Olsen into the tradition of the
truly revolutionary writers such as Tolstoy, Gorki, and
Chekhov, and away from the existential tradition which
gathers its life spark from a fiery and futile rebellion against
what is perceived as an unalterably anguished human condi-
tion, a tradition into which not only Camus's rebel falls, but
many of those who considered themselves realists and activ-
ists during the thirties.

During the thirties when Tillie Olsen came of age as a
writer, both poverty and sense of the need to alter our soci-

ety touched many who had been previously untouched.
There was a solidarity in the struggle which broke down the
barriers between people and broke through the mounting
existential loneliness and feeling of detachment that had
been building among American expatriates who had fled to
Europe during the twenties, who were now returning because of the depression abroad. In order to get to know their
country again, these expatriates began to travel and to talk to
people. With WPA funds, artists, writers, and filmmakers
were sent to record lives that had previously remained unspoken and unseen. Suddenly there were photographs of
people who had never been photographed before. People
who had never been to the theater before began to see plays
and to create them.

The documentary became a serious art form at this time,
allowing those who did not have literary training to move
from the experience of reading into writing through recording. Thus an enormous "literature of the people" sprang up,
cutting across class and ethnic and political backgrounds.
Yet after the thirties, many of the more established writers
who had been most militant turned away from the cause.
Tillie Olsen did not.

I think it is important in rereading the literature of the
thirties to look closely at what we consider to represent
belief and disillusionment, and to draw distinctions between
those writers whose involvement in the need for basic
change is deeply organic and those who merely sought, in a
violent, essentially hopeless Sorelian struggle, an existential
panacea to a loneliness and detachment they experienced as
inevitable. I think it is essential to draw the distinction between the books of hope and action of the thirties, and those
of energetic anguished battle, in which change is seen as an
existential impossibility.

"I could never have been eligible for inclusion in *The God
That Failed*," Tillie Olsen told me, "because for me it never
was a God and it never failed. I was an atheist's daughter

from the beginning." There also never was a time when she
didn't have a firsthand knowledge of oppression and of revolutionary tradition. Her parents had participated in the 1905
democratic upheavals against the czar in Russia. When these
were suppressed, they emigrated to this country. They settled first on a farm in Nebraska, but soon moved to the city
of Omaha, where her father became the state secretary of the
Socialist Party. Tillie Olsen was born in 1912 or 1913 and
was exposed early to the language of the great socialist
orators, some of whom would stay at her house when they
came to attend meetings in town. She remembers how she
sat on Eugene Victor Debs's lap and was one of three little
girls chosen to give him red roses when he spoke at the town
hall. She remembers how he said that "under Socialism society would be like a great symphony with each person playing his own instrument." When guests would come to their
house, the children would have to sleep on chairs, two, three,
four or even five chairs—depending upon how old the children were at the time—lined up next to one another. Old
copies of the *Comrade,* a magazine which reprinted democratic and revolutionary art and classics from around the
world as well as literature from the native American populist
and socialist movements came to her house. It was through
Upton Sinclair's *Cry For Justice,* most of which was taken from
the *Comrade,* that Tillie Olsen had her first exposure to contemporary European literature and art in reproduction. "It
was a rich childhood from the standpoint of ideas," Tillie
Olsen told me. But economic struggle was constant. There
was never a time when she was not doing something "to
help the family out economically." When she was ten, she
used to work after school shelling peanuts. And since she
was the oldest of six children, she was always taking care of
someone younger. She remembers from an extremely early
age that sense of never having enough time which has
haunted her for most of her life, that sense of most women

and her own mother feeling starved for time. It was only because she was sick a great deal—she had all of the childhood diseases, even scarlet fever—that she had any time at all to read and write. She used to hate winter because she always had a running nose, one of the many things that made her feel self-conscious when, one of the few out of her neighborhood, she "crossed the tracks" to attend Omaha's only academic high school. There a beloved teacher who introduced her to Shakespeare and Edna St. Vincent Millay and to the prose rhythms in Sir Thomas Browne, De Quincy, and Coleridge, made sure that she was present when Carl Sandburg came to town to read and play on his guitar. She later wrote parodies of Sandburg's poetry which she gave to the teacher as "new poems of Sandburg." She wanted this erudite person to be her friend and tried too hard. Eventually the teacher hit her in the forehead with a book over a misunderstanding around the meaning of Hamlet's talking to his dead father. Although Central High School stimulated her intellectually, she felt that it crucified her socially, setting up "hidden injuries of class."

As a child she stuttered. Therefore she kept quiet and listened a great deal. She loved to listen to the language of those around her, the speech of the powerful socialist orators who had such a profound influence on her own use of language, revealing to her early how language was able to affect and move people, the language of the immigrants who did not yet know all of the words they needed in order to express themselves, who had to somehow make do with the words they did know, stretching them, the language of the working people. "The people of the packing-house strike were not masters of language," she told me, "but when they would get up to speak, they would speak with such beauty . . . the sodders, the sod farmers used the language of the prairie when it was all grass and no trees, wind. . . ." She was also deeply affected by the language of her black neigh-

bors and schoolmates, the language that she returns to in
"Oh Yes," with its rhythms that she could not fully enter, yet
longed for. "Very early that chasm between us began, which
books opened up for me," she told. She spoke to me movingly about how she watched the "lessening" of the human
beings with whom she lived in an everyday way, her schoolmates, her neighbors, those in her family, of how even very
early she sensed that harming and impairing of capacity
happening in herself as well.

Very early books became a passion. She remembers the
Kansas published Haldeman Julius 5¢ Blue Books designed
to be small enough to be buttoned into a workingman's shirt
pocket, which seemed to reprint everything one might want
to read. Millions were published in the twenties. Then there
was Harriet Monroe and *Poetry: A Magazine of Verse*. Again
with her sense of urgency about time, she taught herself to
become a speed reader. She kept pushing herself at this task,
until she was able to read a book in fifteen minutes. Then
she decided that she would read every book in the fiction,
poetry, and biography section of the Omaha public library,
beginning with the As. She would pick up a book and read a
couple of pages, and if she didn't like it, she would move on
to the next. The librarian, she later found out, was Willa
Cather's niece. They had a rather ambivalent relationship,
Tillie Olsen remembers, but she was allowed to have adult
reading privileges early. And even though she often ne-
glected to bring books back on time, or, eating an apple right
down to the core, she would let seeds drop on the pages,
those reading privileges were never rescinded. It was during
those years that she also "made a few literary friends." She
met John Neihardt, the poet laureate of Nebraska who wrote
Black Elk Speaks. But most of her life was centered about the
purely practical necessities of survival. In 1931, at the age of
eighteen, she joined the Young Communist League. This
too she sees as a primarily practical decision. "I was one of

millions of kids who had the problem of survival," she told me. "I couldn't live on my family. Probably between 1934 and 1936 or '37, a million joined the party."

"In the very early days of the Depression," she went on, "in 1931 and '32 and '33, when a third of the nation was ill-housed, ill-clothed, ill-nourished, there were a million people riding the boxcars, most of them young, the homeless youth. Nobody wrote an 'on the road' for our generation. The family behind us cooked and killed their dog to eat. Those were the Hoover years of no welfare, do nothingism, and denial, when there were long, long lines and apples, everything that people know about now in that shadowy mythical way. . . ." She stopped.

Yonnondio was to be that "on the road" for the thirties that nobody ever wrote, as well as a kind of portrait of the artist as a young woman for that particular generation. Tillie Olsen first began to write it in late February of 1932 when she was nineteen years old, "to show what a criminal system this was, and what this did to human beings." Begun at the same time Tillie Olsen's first baby was born, she describes it as having "come out of the colleges of motherhood, of everyday work, of human struggle bursting the thick wall of self, as it went on." Deliberately she had chosen to focus on the family because she felt that it was only there that one could really see how social forces and social circumstances limit and shape what one can do. She spoke of how seldom one finds in literature "that realistic knowledge of what happens in human beings, what it is that really shapes or misshapes human beings in our society."

I had said something about the relationship of a creative core of self to the social forces of the times. "Core of self," she cried out in sudden anger. "It is irrelevant to even talk of the core of self when circumstances do not sustain its expression or development, when life has tampered with it and harmed it." Then she spoke of her sense of "the many who

appeared with a few poems or short stories in the publications of the thirties such as the *Anvil* and *New Masses,* who
foundered and were never heard of again."

The thirties brought a rush of internationalism. There was
a feeling of connection to people's struggles the world over,
in Africa, in the Philippines, in Guatemala, El Salvador,
Chile, and Asia. Some of this came from the literature,
through the poetry of Pablo Neruda, Lu Hsun, the "Chinese
Chekhov" of the movement for democracy in Japan's
twenties, through the writings of Ding Ling, of José Rizal, of
writers in translation from many countries. The walls between people, the barriers, the misunderstandings were not
present among those who were deeply immersed in those
times. Tillie Olsen told me about how she wore cotton
stockings that wrinkled, instead of silk stockings, "to tell
Japan to halt the invasion of China."

From 1932 to 1933 Tillie Olsen shuttled back and forth
between Faribault, Minnesota, and Minneapolis, writing
Yonnondio. She remembers that she wrote the first few
chapters comparatively rapidly, along with having her first
baby and "having a rough time of it." In the spring of 1933
she moved to Stockton, California, then to Venice, and then
back. "When you didn't pay your rent you just moved," she
explained. "There was a lot of wandering up and down
California in those days." In 1934, the first chapter of *Yonnondio* was published in the second issue of *Partisan Review,*
under the title of "The Iron Throat." It was hailed as "a work
of an early genius" by Robert Cantwell in *New Republic*
which later published "Thousand Dollar Vagrant," her article describing her arrest and the arrest of others during the
San Francisco General Strike. During this period she worked
putting out the *Waterfront/Worker* and was on board ship a
great deal, holding odd jobs around the clock. "The Strike,"
a poetic prose piece published also in 1934 by *Partisan Review* begins:

"Do not ask me to write of the strike and the terror," she writes. "I am on a battlefield, and the increasing stench and smoke sting the eyes so it is impossible to turn them back into the past. You leave me only this night to drop the bloody garment of Todays, to cleave through the gigantic events that have crashed one upon the other, to the first beginning."

That year she also published two poems in the *Daily Worker*. "I want you women up north to know" (a lament for the plight of the Mexican-American women garment workers) and "There is a lesson" (a memorial poem for the Austrian socialists killed by the new Nazi puppet regime).

Because of the enormous promise shown in the first chapter of *Yonnondio,* and also because of the publicity surrounding her arrest, publishers began to look for Tillie Olsen. Bennett Cerf and Donald Klopfer, who established Modern Library and had just established Random House, offered her a monthly stipend in return for turning out a finished chapter every month. She sent her daughter home to relatives and went to Los Angeles to work, but she found that she felt very separated from the kind of human beings she was closest to, and from her own child. In Hollywood Left circles, she was considered a curiosity, although she does remember fondly her meeting with Tess Slesinger with whom she had one of her "few literary conversations."

During those years from time to time she went back to Stockton and other Central Valley towns for three or four day stretches to help organize the agricultural workers. For a while she lived in a section of Los Angeles that was largely Mexican and Jewish. But soon she gave up her contract and moved back to San Francisco. She felt like a terrible failure at the time, she told me, for not having finished the novel. Some thirty-eight years later, looking back at the rough drafts and trying to figure out where she was when she wrote them "by what they are typed on and what notebooks and pencils [she] used," she realized that most of her best writing was done after she moved back to San Francisco, when she was living alone with her daughter. The strike story I have quoted here ends with the image of a pregnant woman.

> There was a pregnant woman standing on the corner, outlined against the sky, and she might have been a marble, rigid, eternal, expressing some vast and nameless sorrow. But her face was a flame, and I heard her say after a while dispassionately, as if it had been said so many times no accent was needed, "we'll not forget that. We'll pay it back . . . someday" . . .
>
> The rest, the General Strike, the terror, arrests and jail, the songs in the night, must be written some other time, must be written later . . . But there is so much happening now.

These closing words of August 13, 1934 were to be prophetic in the history of Tillie Olsen's writing career. In 1937, she became pregnant with her second child. She began to lead an everyday life more and more as the decade drew on. By the end of the decade, she was twenty-seven years old and had two children. By the mid-thirties she had four. Somewhere along the line she had stopped writing.

It wasn't until 1972 that Tillie Olsen returned to *Yonnondio.* In a note about the book she writes, "Thought long since lost or destroyed, some of its pages were found intermixed with other old papers . . . during the process of searching for another manuscript." Those pages were sent to her at the MacDowell Writer's Colony, where she began to prepare them for publication in what she describes as an "arduous partnership" between that "long ago young writer" of the thirties and her older self. She spoke to me movingly about how the passage of time and the alteration of concerns which came with each new decade made it impossible for her to complete all of her unrealized projects conceived when she was young. And yet the spirit of Tillie Olsen's first writings from the thirties was to resurface each time she broke her silence, in *Tell Me a Riddle,* a short story collection of the fifties, and again in *Silences* in 1979.

The poem which was her earliest thirties publication begins:

> I want you women up north to know
> how those dainty children's dresses you buy at macy's,
>   wannamakers, gimbles, marshall fields,
> are dyed in blood, are stitched in wasting flesh,
> down in San Antonio, "where sunshine spends the
>   winter."

and it ends:

> I want you to know
> when you finger the exquisite hand-made dresses
> what it means, this working from dawn to midnight,
>   on what strange feet the feverish dawn must come
>   to maria, catalina, ambrosa,
> how the malignant fingers twitching over the pallid faces
>   jerk
> them to work,
> and the sun and the fever mount with the day—
>   long plodding hours, the eyes burn like coals, heat
>   jellies the flying fingers
> down comes the night like blindness.
>   long hours more with the dim eye of the lamp, the
>   breaking back,
> weariness crawls in the flesh like worms, gigantic like
>   earth's in winter . . .

> And for twenty eight hundred ladies of joy the grotesque
> act gone over—the wink—the grimace—the "feeling like
> it baby?"

And for Maria Vasquez, spinster, emptiness, emptiness,
   flaming with dresses for children she can never fondle.
And for Ambrosa Espinoza—the skeleton body of her
   brother on his mattress of rags, boring twin holes in the
   dark with his eyes to the image of christ, remembering
   a leg, and twenty-five years cut off from his life by the
   railroad.

Women up north, I want you to know
I tell you this can't last forever

I swear it won't.

There is no redeeming voice in the poem until the cry, "I
tell you this can't last forever. I swear it won't." This final
cry becomes the call to action, while the body of the poem
constitutes an insistence that we enter fully into the dark
terror of conditions as they are in order that we come out
caring enough to change them. Because the setting of *Yonnondio* is equally bleak, yet much of the story is told by a still
hopeful child, there is a kind of fugue and counterfugue
around the undeniable heavy presence of so much darkness
and discouragement, and what it means to stay awake
enough in the face of that dark existence to eventually gather
the energy to alter it.

   "I would be a-cryen," Mazie, the child, whispers to herself
in the prologue to one of the most searing "initiation" scenes
I have encountered in fiction, "but all the tears is stuck inside
me. All the world is a-cryen and I don't know for why. And
the ghosts may get daddy. Now he's goin away, but he'll
come back with something sweet but sicklike hangin on his
breath, and hit momma and start the baby a-bawlen. If it was
all a dream, if I could only just wake up and daddy'd be
smilin, and momma laughin, and us playing."

   In the scene that follows the child will lie down on the
rising black slag heap to watch the sunset, letting the ecstacy

of its colors enter her, "Like babies tongues, like what happens to the backs of your eyes when you close em after seeing the sun, only that hurts." The fiery beauty of the sunset will begin to soothe and to put into place the frightening fragments of memories of mine disasters and domestic strife, the sense of poverty and being stifled. The wind will come "flinging the fine bits of coal dust from the culm against her face, . . . reminding her of the rough hand of her father when he caressed her, hurting her, but not knowing it, hurting with a pleasant hurt."

Because the opening chapter of *Yonnondio,* written when Tillie Olsen was nineteen, is told primarily through the consciousness of children trying to put together the pieces of a badly shattered and oppressive world, both the surge toward letting go to the human spirit and the tragedy of repression, the battering of the System, becomes more pronounced. For even when Tillie Olsen leaps out of the voices of the children into those of the adults surrounding them, the themes of the crushing of the spirits of children remain foremost, the children becoming simultaneously the symbol of the actualization of the hope the adults cannot dare to nurture except during rare exalted moments when a "clearing" is able to come. And yet this is one of the few books in which we can watch vividly adults hurting children without hating them. Instead our hatred turns toward the System that crushes and contorts all of life, leaving the span of striving so brief.

Thus as we go from Mazie's mind, as she lies watching the sunset on the culm, into the mind of the drunken man damaged by a mine explosion who sees her and mistakes her frail white body fluttering against the blackness of the culm for an angel, we are brought almost lovingly into the heart of the Terror Tillie Olsen writes about in her strike story, as the demented man picks up the child Mazie to feed her to the mine that has been devouring too many men.

That was it. The mine was hungry for a child, she was reaching her thousand arms for it. "She only takes men 'cause she ain't got kids."

"Give her a sweet baby, and she'll want no more." Angels singing, men, strong-bodied men, marching and singing, saved. Her body, soft, trembled against him. Ecstacy sang. Now the shaft, hungry mouth.

"I am giving you your baby."

Although Mazie is saved by a mine guard who intervenes and kills the man instead, plunging him into the mine shaft he had feared, the incident will be indelibly imprinted both in Mazie's consciousness and our own. This combined initiation into sexuality and the awareness of death which comes to all adolescents, but came to Mazie too early and in a mangled form, will sow the seeds for a political awareness eventually to come. For here, and throughout *Yonnondio,* the deepest source of the cruelty we see comes not from the individuals who perpetrate it, nor from death and sexual desire seen as evil "supernatural" forces we cannot control, but rather from the needless warping of those same, basically good and very natural forces by a System that *can* be avoided, that *can* be changed.

Yonnondio is very much a book about human work, both paid and unpaid, work seen simultaneously in its largest and in its most essential, most daily sense. Each year, Tillie Olsen told me, the book becomes more popular, for there is a real need for serious exploration of such themes in our literature. As the decade of *Yonnondio*'s conception drew on, and Tillie Olsen's social and political consciousness deepened, her need to write about the world of work grew greater. Simultaneously, through having children of her own, in the later portions of the book, she moves more and more into the consciousness of the adults.

Into her great physical pain and weariness Anna stumbled and lost herself. Remote she fed and clothed the children, scrubbed, gave herself to Jim, clenching her fists against a pain she had no strength to feel. In the front room Jimmie played and sang to himself, falling asleep when she didn't come for him, wetting his overalls when she forgot.

Bess, the baby, starts to sicken.

"gettin blue around the mouth and squalls all the time now."

But she could not really care. Only sometimes, nursing the baby, chafing the little hands to warm them, old songs would start from her lips and tears well from her eyes, tears she did not even know she was weeping, till Ben would come in, standing lacerated till she would notice him and ask, "What's the matter, Benjy, did you hurt yourself?" and he would come over to her and say gently, "Mommy, you're crying."

And Jim. . . . He was padded about with weariness, he was blinded with despair.

Jim's sense of his own masculinity is seriously shaken when a younger, less burdened man stands up to the bosses. Out of the cold impatience of his complaining to Anna about her kitchen world, his seeming outer cruelty, rises this sudden monologue which years later was picked up as the subject of performance by three "kids" at the Ozark Arts Festival who found that it spoke so strongly to their own reality.

Alright for Tracy to talk, alright, he didn't have a wife and kids hangin around his neck like an anchor. . . . Tracy was young, just twenty, still wet behind the ears and the old blinders were on him so he couldn't really see what was around and he believed the bull about freedom of opportunity and a chance to rise and if you really want to work you can always find a job and rugged individualism and something about pursuit of happiness . . .

He didn't know . . . So he threw it up, not yet knowing a job was God, he renounced God, he became an atheist and suffered the tortures of the damned, and God Job (being full up that generation) never took him back into the fold only a few days at a time, and he learned all right what it meant to be an infidel . . .

He learned all right, the tortures of the damned: feet slapping the pavement, digging humbly into carpets, squatting wide apart in front of chairs and the nojobnojob nothingdointoday buzzing in his ears; eking the coffee—and out; shuffling along the frozen streets, buddy (they made a song out of it) can you spare a dime, and the freights north east south west, getting vagged, keep movin, keep movin (the bulls don't need to tell ya your own belly yells it out, your own idle hands) *sing a song* of hunger the weather four below holes in your pockets and nowhere to go, the flophouses, the slophouses, a bowl of misery and last month's cruller, and the crabs having a good time spreading and spreading (you didn't know hell would be this bad, did you?).

Oh he learned alright . . . Many are Called but Few Are Chosen, and are not the Sins of the Fathers (having nothing to sell but their labor power) Visited on the Sons . . . He learned alright, alright, that last hour writhing in the "piano" in the chain gang down in Florida.

And there's nothing to say, Jim Tracy, I'm sorry, Jim Tracy, sorry as hell we weren't stronger and

could get to you in time and show you that kind of
individual revolt was no good, kid, no good at all,
you had to bide your time and take it till there were
enough of you to fight it all together on the job, and
bide your time, and take it till the day millions of
fists clamped in yours, and you could wipe out the
whole thing, the whole goddamn thing, and a human could be a human for the first time on earth.

Often in *Yonnondio,* at times such as this, the fictional form
breaks out of itself into passages that are half poem and half
essay, functioning as an intensely Whitmanesque universal
ground from which the individual histories and monologues
rise in a swell of feeling and into which, when spent, the
purely personal must return, "Yonnondio! Yonnondio!—
unlimn'd they disappear," the Whitman poem that forms the
opening monograph fulfilling itself slowly as the book unfolds, the writing reaches a poetic climax and rhythmic "perfection" in which the form completely echoes the content in
the sections about Jim's assembly line in the meat packing-
house, and Anna in her kitchen which lead into the final dust
storm, which brings the book to an end.

> Hell.
> Choreographed by Beedo,* the B system, speed-
> up stopwatch, convey. Music by rasp crash screech
> knock steamhiss thud machinedrum. Abandon self,
> all ye who enter here. Become component part,
> geared, meshed, timed, controlled.
> Hell. Figures half-seen through hissing vapor,
> live steam cloud from great scalding vats. Hogs dan-
> gling, dancing along the convey, 300, 350 an hour;
> Mary running running along the rickety platform to
> keep up, stamping, stamping the hides. To

*Beedo: A speed-up system of the 1920s.

the shuddering drum of the skull crush machine, in
the spectral vapor clouds, everyone the same motion
all hours through: Kryckszi lifting his cleaver, the
one powerful stroke; long continuous arm swirl of
the rippers, gut pullers, Marsalek pulling leaf lard,
already faint in the sweated heat, breathing with
open mouth.

Breathing with open mouth, the young girls and
women in Casings, where men will not work.

. . .

In Casings it is 110°. A steam kettle, thinks Ella,
who has a need to put things into words, a steam
kettle, and in a litany: *steamed, boiled, broiled, fried,
cooked: steamed, boiled, broiled, fried, cooked* . . .

In the hog room, 108°. Kerchiefs, bound around
foreheads to keep the salt sweat from running down
into eyes and blinding, become saturated; each
works in a rain of stinging sweat . . .

Slow it, we got to slow it . . .

Interspersed through the poetic repetition of these facts of
the external conditions in the packinghouse, Tillie Olsen
weaves for us an escalating surging of the tales and feelings
of the people we have come to know throughout the book,
the familiar taking on a new pitch of intensity and power that
is both personal and political.

In the humid kitchen, Anna works alone. . . . The
last batch of jelly is on the stove. Between stirring
and skimming, and changing the wet packs on Ben,
Anna peels and cuts the canning peaches—two more
lugs to go. If only all will sleep a while. She begins
to sing softly—I saw a ship a-sailing, a-sailing on
the sea—it clears her head. The drone of the fruit
flies and Ben's rusty breathing are very loud in the
unmoving, heavy air. Bess begins to fuss again.
There, there, Bessie, there, there.

Somehow, through all the struggle and the actual hardship, the human spirit, the spirit of work and caring, tri-
umphs, even in those most trodden down.

"Conceived primarily as a novel of the 1930s," Tillie
Olsen writes in her closing note to the published version of
Yonnondio, "unfinished, it yet bespeaks the consciousness and
roots of that decade, if not its actual events." For the book
did not actually live long enough to extend many years
beyond its opening in the early twenties in a small Wyo-
ming mining town. The children never did grow up to become the orphans and Communist organizers they were
meant to be, and yet, perhaps for that very reason, because it
is so much a book about that "sense of human potential" so
central to Tillie Olsen's life philosophy and so essential to
what was most noble in firing the political activity of the
thirties, the very unfinished, not-yet-grown-up quality of
this book, the fact that it does not arrive even into the onset
of the era that claims to be about, yet is perpetually moving
in that direction, renders it, in impact—if not realized form
and content—the very epic it was meant to be.

Because the futures of the characters seemed still so
alive in Tillie Olsen as she began to reminisce about them, I
asked her if she was ever tempted to continue writing about
them. She said yes, but that each decade of lives, each era
brings forth its own concerns which necessarily take priority.
Only once in the late forties, after the bombing of Hiroshima, she found herself recording a strong image of herself
and the decay, of "ashes to ashes and dust to dust, and winds
endlessly blowing the dust that had been Anna and Mazie
and Jim, endless terrible dust storms swirling in my head."

The part of *Yonnondio* that would have come next, had she
continued to write it at the time, was the strike. Jim, the
father, was going to abandon the family and Anna, the
mother, was going to have to face her pregnancy alone. The
grocer would refuse to give the family credit, Anna would
lose her teeth, and attempt to find out where to get an abor-

tion. "Being a young writer, I killed Anna off," Tillie Olsen said. Mazie was given a job in which she was sexually abused. "I had it all outlined, chapter by chapter. Ben—I'm afraid I may have been influenced by Victorian children—dies. But not sentimentally." She explained to me that what so many modern critics misunderstand as sentimentality around the deaths of children in Victorian fiction was actually a response to previous centuries in which child mortality was taken for granted, an inability to accept it any longer as God's will. This brought an anguish over the deaths of so many young children, as well as a different sense of the value of the individual child. "It was the first period that children were mourned in that particular way."

After Ben dies the children are dispersed. The couple in the beginning of *Yonnondio* take in Jimmy. Baby Bess goes to an orphanage. Mazie and Will return to the close relationship they had in early childhood, and become part of the homeless youth on their way to California. Will—this was a 1934 outline—becomes one of the young organizers and joins the Communist Party, or so she envisioned it according to her early notes.

Tillie Olsen spoke to me about how "the writer that she is now" mourns the loss of the knowledge that she was amassing in those years in which she didn't have the time or means to record it. "That is part of the problem when work is deferred," she said. As the years went on she felt that she would have tried to keep the family together, that maybe she would have not killed off Ben. Her feeling about the Communist Party also changed. "Towards the end of the thirties," she said, "I don't know . . . I had a different understanding of the ways in which the party was so wrong in how it handled people." She had ceased being a party member. Although through activities, classes, and events themselves, so many people grew within the party, she saw also the limitations of a structure which "did not allow for a development from actual United States events and needs."

And yet she still believes that "put into a larger context, the Communist Party policy to try to prevent World War II, to stop the fascist Nazi powers and colonialization, was far more often correct than any other international policy, and that for years domestically it was the fueling force for essential changes such as the establishment of social security, welfare, and union organization. She told me that she never became disillusioned in that she never stopped believing in human beings' capacity to make necessary changes by working together while simultaneously life continued to remind her of how difficult any human ventures are, even individual relationships and families, let alone political movements.

I asked why Steinbeck had turned away after the thirties. She told me that the struggles of the farmworkers went on just as dramatically in Salinas Valley and elsewhere throughout the forties, the fifties, the sixties, the seventies, and still, only Steinbeck and others were not watching. As an aside she commented that the fame and the Nobel Prize "were not because of *Grapes of Wrath,* but because of the millions of human beings who made struggles of this kind and themselves visible. Remember, if not for the struggles of the thirties," she said, "and the interests they created, and the WPA Writers' Project, many books, photographs, and films would never have come into being. James Agee and Walker Evans would never have gone south and given us their imperishable *Let Us Now Praise Famous Men.* They, almost alone, brought to their work the rare mixture of quality, identification, and torment—torment because they knew they were only 'tourists'; they would write the book, go back to their privileged life, and leave the people about whom they wrote in their unchanged lives."

Silences, Tillie Olsen's latest book, which came out in 1979, begins with the dedication:

For our silenced people, century after century their beings consumed in the hard, everyday essential work of maintaining human life. Their art, which still they made—as their other contributions—anonymous, refused respect, recognition lost.

and

For those of us (few yet in number, for the way is punishing), their kin and descendants, who begin to emerge into more flowered and rewarded use of our selves in ways denied to them;—and by our achievement bearing witness to what was (and still is) being lost, silenced.

Literary history and the present are dark with silences; some of the silences for years by our acknowledged great; some silences hidden; some the ceasing to publish after one work appears; some the never coming to book form at all.

These are not natural silences, that necessary time for renewal, lying fallow, gestation, in the natural cycle of creation. The silences I speak of here are unnatural; the unnatural thwarting of what struggles to come into being, but cannot. In the old, the obvious parallels: when the seed strikes stone; the soil will not sustain; the spring false; the time is drought or blight infestation; the frost comes premature.

This book . . . is concerned with the relationship of circumstances—including class, color, sex, the times, climate into which one is born—to the creation of literature . . .

Silences is half a nonfiction essay, half a long prose poem, a collaging of words of other writers on the subject with her own. Then suddenly, out of its center rises like an extraordinary beacon of light, a resurrection of Rebecca Harding Da-

vis, whose "Life in the Iron Mills" or "The Korl Woman"
appeared anonymously in the *Atlantic* in April of 1861, who
enjoyed for a brief moment the support and friendships of
the Hawthornes and Oliver Wendell Holmes and Emerson,
before her own life took her back into darkness and oppression once again, before she was forgotten. Tillie Olsen had
found the story in an old bound copy of *Atlantic* reprints
when she was fifteen years old, but it wasn't until 1958,
when she came across a reference to it in one of Emily
Dickinson's letters that she discovered who the author was.
She brought the book to the attention of the Feminist Press,
which published it along with her writings about it.

Now merged forever with my images of Mazie in the
sunset lying on the rising mountain of black slag will always
be the earlier image of Rebecca Harding Davis's man, who,
in the lurid flaming iron pits, makes from the iron shards
("korl,") a statue of a woman hungry and hoping, an eerie
apparition of what people can create if they are given a
chance, standing out forever in my memory against the hell-
like flames. Now it is Ding Ling, "who lived out Mao's
words that art must serve the people, that art must create a
new kind of human being," whose works Tillie Olsen would
like to bring forward to the public consciousness.

"Time on the bus, even when I had to stand, was enough;
the stolen moments at work, enough, the deep night hours
for as long as I could stay awake, after the kids were in bed,
after the household tasks were done, sometimes during. It is
no accident that the first work I considered publishable began: 'I stand here ironing, and what you ask me moves
tormented back and forth with the iron.'"

Tillie Olsen's collected stories ("I Stand Here Ironing,"
"Hey Sailor, What Ship," "Oh Yes," and "Tell Me a
Riddle"), which came out in 1956, would form the subject
for an essay in themselves, for the fifties were "a very different time" in this country, and each of the stories surges with

so much that just must be said. It is impossible to do them justice here without wandering very far away from the thirties. Every time I reread the stories and experience anew just how much can be contained in a tiny space (for none of the stories are long), I am amazed at how a lifetime of caring about other people, will, and passion bursts out of every word that is expressed as well as out of the spaces between the words. I am amazed at what happens when suddenly the dry earth cracks and the spring gushes forth, at how once again the passion of the making of the thirties comes up full blown out of the fifties' brutal shell.

The first time I saw Tillie Olsen in April of 1981 she was reading "Tell Me a Riddle" at the 92nd Street YMHA. A movie had just been made of it. I remember how her voice rose and fell with the emotional fluctuations of the material. Unfolding image upon image, memory upon memory, she let her voice range over the richness of her own language, almost screaming sometimes, almost singing sometimes, with a marvelous Heraclitian flow. But from time to time, she would interrupt herself and begin to talk about what she had written. Then she would start to stutter again, as she had when she was a child; she let the audience into the private world of her own emotional reactions to her material. She was reading about Eva, the old grandmother whose song had been shattered and sucked dry, reading what she had written during the repressive reign of McCarthy, when suddenly she interrupted herself, right before the grandmother was to die, to return to the ending of the published version of *Yonnondio* in which the baby Bess bangs a jar lid in celebration of all the hope yet to be born.

> *Bang!*
> Bess who had been fingering a fruit-jar lid—absently, heedlessly dropped it—aimlessly groping across the table, reclaims it again. Lightning in her

brain. She releases, grabs, releases, grabs. I can do. Bang! I did that. I can do! I! A look of neanderthal concentration is on her face. That noise! In triumphant, astounded joy she clashes the lid down. Bang, slam, whack. Release, grab, slam, bang, bang. Centuries of human drive work in her; human ecstacy of achievement; satisfaction deeper and more fundamental than sex: I can do, I use my powers; I! I!

And she spoke of how she believed that we were all that baby once, with all of human potential and wonder, and all possibility in us, the human baby, the only proof we have so far that we are all the human race, how she believed that we could all become that baby still. I will never forget that moment. Nor will I forget Tillie Olsen's own silence that night after she finished reading. For easily ten minutes she and the audience shared their reactions to her story in a silence in which every fluctuation of her face spoke. I can hear that thirties' baby's jar lid banging in that silence still.

MERIDEL LE SUEUR

*W*hat does an American think about the land, what dreams come from the sight of it, what painful dreaming? Are they only money dreams, power dreams? . . . Remember the sadness and innate depression of Lincoln as symbolic. He was naturally a lover, but he never loved the land, although he walked miles over it, slept and lived on it, and buried the bodies of those he loved in it; and yet he was never struck with that poetry and passion that makes a man secure upon his land, there was always instead the convulsion of anxiety, this fear. . . . I remembered Lincoln's body, hard and bitter and stubborn, always lanky and ill-nourished, surviving bitterly.

The words of Meridel Le Sueur's 1930 story "Corn Village" came back to me as I watched her deliver the keynote address for the 1981 American Writers' Congress, sponsored by the Nation Institute. I will not forget her presence as she stood on the podium set up in the gaudy Grand Ballroom of New York City's Roosevelt Hotel, talking about the struggle of the writer during the depression. Crowded into the Grand Ballroom hung with crimson cur-

tains and enormous crystal chandeliers were 3,000 writers from all over the United States who came to hear this "survivor" call for a return of the power over the written word to the people. Meridel Le Sueur was dressed sedately in black, but her white hair had a regal glow against the white bric-a-brac of the hotel walls. She was talking about rebirth, about seeding and sprouting.

Blacklisted for more than thirty years, her works only available in contraband pamphlets given out on picket lines or kept behind the counter in small midwestern butcher shops and grocery stores, Meridel Le Sueur had been hoisted into a position of sudden celebrity by the unlikely union of old-time leftists, feminists interested in resurrecting matriarchal roots, political thinkers, advocates of working-class writing, and lovers of the poetic lore of the midwest. Out of a position of relative obscurity, she is now being made into a cult figure—her work, her presence, and the particular progression of her art from social realism to a feminist celebration of fertility becoming emblematic of our era.

Meridel Le Sueur came of age as a writer in the 1930s in the heyday of the reemergence of the populist and workers' movements. Her short stories about poor people, strikes, and women and babies appeared frequently in the *New Masses* and the *Daily Worker,* as well as in the *American Mercury, Partisan Review,* the *Nation, Scribner's,* and other journals. They won the enthusiastic praise of Sinclair Lewis, Horace Gregory, Nelson Algren, and Carl Sandburg, who wrote of how she was "moved by the tremendous themes of the modern world which suffuse her work with a rather rare quality of reverence for humanity, of intimacy and pride regarding women and motherhood." Sandburg described her as "an original artist beautifully reverent, with a high solemnity, gravely achieved affirmations of life, an approach too infrequent among the realist and naturalist schools of writers. . . . She is a witness with a genius for moving and highly implicative testimony."

I felt that Meridel Le Sueur was once again bearing witness as she stood before the assembled writers of the congress, calling to mind the political writers of the thirties who
had attended the original writers' congresses about bread
and butter issues during the depression, reciting their names,
legendary by now, writers who were also blacklisted, long
vanished, so many of them already dead, and she still alive,
still interested in new political movements and new literary
styles, still traveling around the country by airplane and by
Greyhound bus, reading her works and talking to people,
especially to women, still organizing. She seemed to have
been everywhere in the past few months, in her own state of
Minnesota at a People's Theater convention, in Texas at a
women's ritual to reclaim the yarns of women's daily lives,
in Lincoln, Nebraska at a school of Indian languages. Like
the spirit of Joe Hill, she seemed invincible, irrepressible,
omnipresent. No matter how, in the future, *they* might attempt to kill her and the power of her message, I cannot help
feeling that she will reappear forever, wherever there is
work and organizing needing to be done. Born at the turn of
the century, now turning eighty-two years old, she is more
active than almost any younger person I can think of.

During the week that followed her keynote address, she
was hard at work participating in special forums on censor-
ship and on working-class writing, puzzling out ways in
which to found a people's press and distribution system,
helping to plan a writer's union, meeting with the women
from the Feminist Press who were in the process of putting
together a comprehensive anthology of her works. She was
staying with Adelaide Bean, the editor of "Page Eight," the
entertainment page of the *Daily World.*

When I first came to call on Meridel Le Sueur, Adelaide
Bean refused to let me see her. "If only I knew you were
coming," Adelaide Bean said by way of a greeting, "I would
have tried to prevent it. They all keep coming and she really

has to rest." She stood resolutely in the doorway of her cozy eat-in kitchen, barricading my way. And looking at her, I couldn't help thinking of the women of Meridel Le Sueur's strike stories.

"I will go home and call another day," I volunteered. But Adelaide Bean was implacable. Adroitly she changed places with me, so that her body, which one minute earlier was guarding the entrance, was now guarding the egress. I liked her immediately. "You can't come back another day," she said with a fierceness I could only admire. "She hasn't another minute to see anybody." She put her arms outward in the shape of a picket-line fence. She had her grey hair tied in a knot at the top of her neck. Her face was beautiful, worn, strong, reminding me of the faces of the women of Kathe Kollwitz's drawings, as do all of Meridel Le Sueur's women. As she walked away to the back bedroom to awaken her charge, I noticed again the Kollwitz-like strength and serenity of her gestures. I noticed the regal way her garments flowed, a graphic monument to her proud resignation in the face of all the work yet waiting to be done. And I thought again of the women in Meridel Le Sueur's strike stories, washing tin coffee cups at union meetings, washing babies' bottoms, washing police-inflicted buckshot wounds. I felt comforted and reassured to be there. I was granted exactly an hour by Adelaide Bean, who ushered me in with a sigh.

Meridel Le Sueur lay on a narrow bed, dressed in a brilliant scarlet blouse. She was using a black silk quilted jacket as a cover for her feet. When she rose to a sitting position to greet me, motioning to a chair beside the bed, the big beaded horse that she wore around her neck seemed to gallop along with her rising, and jiggle and sway, its hair-tail flying. Her long, white hair was parted in the middle and pinned back. She was part Indian, I had been told, though whether that was really so, I never did find out. Only later, when I had absorbed the whole of Meridel Le Sueur's trajectory, did I realize the importance of the answer to this question. It was one of the characteristics of this writer of so much straightforward first-person narrative, that she talked very little about herself in a straightforward way. I came away with a great deal of essence, and very little fact.

Her feet were encased in brown suede moccasins. "Do you mind if I put them up?" she asked. "It seems that the feet are the first part of us to go." She continued looking at her feet thoughtfully. "We rot from the bottom up," she said. "The rest of me is doing fine." Then she asked me how many miles I thought a person walked in a lifetime. It was not a rhetorical question. She really wanted to know what I thought. When I didn't answer back, she ventured her own opinion. "I would think it must be about three times around the world," she said. She smiled at me.

"The young women today are wonderful," she said. "They are like hens. They brood. They sit on their eggs. They get to the heart of things directly with no holding back." Then she went on to tell me how the brood hen is the most important creature in society. "The hen is more motherly," she said. "She understands the nourishing of something that doesn't exist yet. She understands the hatching. Capitalism was an artificial egg."

Meridel Le Sueur came from a very political family. Her father was the first Socialist mayor of Minto, North Dakota. Her mother ran for senator when she was seventy-four. After Meridel Le Sueur's youngest brother was born, her mother took the children away from their father, out of the state of Texas to a state where women would not be considered as the property of men. Meridel Le Sueur didn't meet her father again until he was ninety and she was fifty. He was still a preacher and had a church in San Antonio. "He had heard about Buddha," she said rather wistfully, leaving the statement to stand on its own as a kind of non sequitur, and she was silent for a minute before she changed the subject to her mother who "was one of the most beautiful women." "All she did wrong was read those books," her father said.

After leaving her father, her mother became a lecturer on the "Chautauqua Circuit," an organized program of political speeches offered to rural people who came and camped out on hillsides throughout the country. Meridel Le Sueur especially remembers her mother's lecture on "Love and Bread" in which her mother contended that "women did not have a choice of love because of the economy of bread." She remembers that once a woman in Kansas City was sentenced to ninety-nine years in prison for using contraceptives. The woman had fourteen children. Meridel Le Sueur's mother took care of them. Meridel Le Sueur was still a child at the time.

"Women were beaten all the time in those days," Meridel Le Sueur said. "Men had horrible lives. The only people that they had to beat were wives. That was when the library began. If you only got men reading, you would do away with sex and drinking. So they had Robert Browning Clubs where they would plant flowers." Meridel Le Sueur didn't hear any music outside of church music until she was eighteen years old. She never saw a hospital, or running water, or electricity.

Her grandmother, she said, was a very brilliant woman. She used to go around with a horse and buggy and a shotgun to get men to stop drinking and beating their wives. She was a member of the Women's Christian Temperance Union, and hated sex. She had had five children, but still didn't seem to understand where they came from. When her grandmother was eighty, Meridel Le Sueur gave her a copy of *Gray's Anatomy*. On the other hand her grandfather, a brilliant, drunken lawyer, started having sex when he was twelve, and then looked around for the most eligible, pure virgin. From the first night it was rape. It was the double standard of those times. Her grandmother thought that men

were victims born with a terrible apparatus, that it was the
mission of women to care for men and save them. Her
grandmother read only biblical tracts, and the only
sanctioned sexual experience was baptism, by the erotic
wandering evangelist who took you in his arms and immersed you under water. And in another nine months, half
of the babies in the village would be born looking just like
him.

"Imagine it," she said. "All of the people are on the bank
singing. And you are in a beautiful white dress. You wade
into the water, and then the handsome evangelist takes you
in his arms and puts you all the way under the water. There
were great orgies after being saved in Indiana and Ohio. A
lot of the nation was begat that way."

When Meridel Le Sueur was ten, she began to write as a
"secret guerrilla action." She began to give plays with "other
women of the village. The white people were of the minority
there. The Mexican and Indian women loved the earth. They
menstruated when they were nine, and had breasts. They
had babies when they were in the sixth grade." She attended
the Indian ceremonials, although her grandmother was
against her "going with them" lest she be corrupted. Her
grandmother also hated her writing. Whenever she would
find it, she would destroy it. "All my life I've concealed the
unsayable," her grandmother would say to her. "Now you're
going to destroy it all by telling it." "When I write I can still
feel her bitter mouth turning down."

As Meridel Le Sueur told me these stories about her
grandmother, I was vividly reminded of her short story
called "Fudge" which I had read on the subway ride up. It is
the story of an adolescent wakening, of a girl's coming of age
in a small and close-lipped town, and of her visit to an older
woman, shrouded in mystery and rage, to whom "something
had happened and then stopped happening. . . .

I heard the story bit by bit, piecing it together and watching Nina Shelley as she moved to her windows, spying back upon the town that had set her like a fly in amber, hardening in her own and their hatred.

I saw her too when she came to church and how there was a hush and a withdrawing from her, for she was a visible sign of their own lust and had now come into the town's dreams, with her urgency that had lasted so short a time. They congealed and flowed around her in their bitterness, she, being sign and symbol, set up for all to see on church day and on market day, coming gruesomely for food for spirit and for body, to feed the corpse they had already buried for her. The women never embraced or touched her, and held her off from their children, from their own warm hearths, glad that she, by her sparsity, made their own bitterness seem abundant and rich.

She was always phoning, asking young girls or young school teachers to come over and see her. Not many would go.

But the Meridel Le Sueur who tells the story does go, thinking "that possibly she had only tried once to step out of herself and that time had curdled and embittered her," and that "malice then would be the cover of pity in her for what she knew to be in the world."

Meridel Le Sueur went to see the frightening old lady because she wanted to see, to know, "to cry out, 'But what really happened? What was it? Warn us. Save us.'" The other girl who had gone with her ran away, but she "didn't run, and in that moment I cracked the meaning in my teeth and the bitterness of it lay in me then. . . . Now it all came from behind what had stood before it and I had to let my lips come over it and know it forever with what I would be able to find out about other things.

She had had a hunger just like me,

she writes, referring to the frightening old Miss Shelley, only

she couldn't do it. She couldn't know. She couldn't risk. She wasn't able. What nobody was knowing, what was standing in that town over Miss Shelley's house was that nothing happened. Nothing happened! Except the wound that she gave to herself, taking a shot at her own breast. And the town's rancor standing equally in them all was that nothing happened in any of them, neither sun, moon, husband, or child broke them open to good growing.

And I remember that standing in the sun I began to cry as if for my own lost life that had not yet begun and yet stood finished before me.

And out of that earliest cry, that mourning for the loss of the experience of life that comes from not loving enough, not risking enough, and not trying hard enough to make something beautiful and important happen, came Meridel Le Sueur's future artistic voice and her courage to struggle to make the world what she wanted it to be.

Her grandmother believed in the straight line, and even her mother told her that she had to learn how to raise cabbages as well as roses. But something in her nature rebelled. "The straight line leads directly to the bomb," she told me. "T.S. Eliot wrote that to William Carlos Williams, did you know that—straw men, hollow men . . . go out with a whimper, not with a bang. *The Waste Land* paralyzed me for several years. It paralyzed a great many of us. People became existentialists. I began to talk against Plato when I was twelve years old. If this is what school is, I said, I'm leaving." She never did go back to school.

In 1928 she had her first child. It was a difficult time to have a child, she told me because people thought that they had been betrayed in the war. And so people went around saying things like "no more children for cannon fodder . . . Not many men wanted to be fathers in those days. I never met any fathers. . . . So I decided to have them on my own. It was like stealing the seed." She paused and fell quiet a bit, thinking. "I needed to have a child. It was like survival. There seems to be a tremendous thing like that among women, so really despairing. Everything seemed to come to an end with the war. I think I would have died. And yet, I don't think you should have a child in order not to commit suicide. I don't think you should want to have a child to solve problems."

I thought of the woman of her short story "Annunciation," waiting alone, heavy-bellied, watching the pear tree, the starving wife of a husband out of a job.

People are driving in and out. But up here it is very quiet and the movement of the pear tree is the only movement and I seem to hear its delicate sound of living as it moves upon itself silently, and outward and upward. . . . I can see it spiraling upwards from below, its stem straight, and from it, spiraling the branches season by season, and from the spiraling branches moving out in quick motion, the forked stems, and from the stems twirling fragilely the tinier stems holding outward until they fall, the half-curled pear leaves. . . . The pear tree from above looks as if it had been shot instantaneously from the ground, shot upward like a rocket to break in showers of leaves and fruits twirling and falling. Its movement looks quick, sudden and rocketing. My child when grown can be looked at in this way as if it suddenly existed . . . but I know the slow time of making. The pear tree knows. . . .

I sit here all the afternoon as if in its branches, midst the gentle and curving body of the tree. I have looked at it until it has become more familiar to me than Karl. It seems a strange thing that a tree might come to mean more to one than one's husband. It seems a shameful thing even. I am ashamed to think of it but it is so. I have sat here in the pale sun and the tree has spoken to me with its many tongued leaves, speaking through the afternoon of how to round a fruit. And I listen through the slow hours. I listen to the whisperings of the pear tree, speaking to me, speaking to me. How can I describe what is said by a pear tree? Karl did not speak to me so. No one spoke to me in any good speech.

There is a woman coming up the stairs, slowly. I can hear her breathing. I can hear her behind me at the screen door.

She came out and spoke to me. I know why she was looking at me so closely. "I hear you're going to have a child," she said. "It's too bad." She is the same color as the dead leaves in the park. Was she once alive too?

We talked a great deal about needing to know the darkness before we can experience the light. "Being down there in the pit," she calls it. She is writing a new novel about women in the pit, in the dark bowels of the earth. "Women don't go up without going down first," she explained. "Women must get in touch with something down there, somewhere in the ground. They must meet there and give birth there. Did you know that there was a whole village of women in Kansas who believed that they were going to give birth to the new messiah. It was like the Dead Sea scrolls. They were wonderful women, agricultural women." I asked her if the messiah was male, and she said that she thought so.

"But maybe women don't ascend at all," she said again after a minute. "You'd hardly catch a woman hanging from a cross." And she told me about her fascination with the fertility of ancient Greece and Crete. "There they had no conception of time between birth and death. They would hold up an ear of corn at the fall solstice. They had no conception of space between the womb and the tomb."

I asked her how she managed during the McCarthy era, how she survived as a writer, but she merely replied, "We never did belong to the establishment you know. We would have known we weren't doing something right, if we weren't attacked." Then I asked her about her relationship with her mother. "Mother and I were very different," she told me, "and very dangerous to one another. She was very active and violent. We were very opposite from one another, and very oppressive to each other. Yet we also honored those positions. I feel I needed her to goose me into action."

Then she told me the tale of a mother bear going through the woods who sees "all these wren's eggs abandoned by the dead mother wren and sits down on them." She told me how her mother "would fight for her children. But she would also smash them." Her mother was a brilliant mathematician who could not study mathematics. She ran for senator when she was seventy-four, in order to speak out against the Korean War.

Meridel Le Sueur talked very fast. "Women today have so much to say to one another," she said. "We must find ways to meet, in a hole in the ground, or in the belly of a hollow tree. We must all get together."

Suddenly I looked at my watch and realized that Adelaide Bean would be back to dismiss me momentarily, and that still, despite the charismatic intensity of our interview, I was lacking the crucial data—names, dates, and places—that would give a coherent framework to my understanding of the history of Meridel Le Sueur's long, complicated life.

"I need some facts," I said rather desperately. "My editor insisted that I bring back facts."

However, Meridel Le Sueur was not to be persuaded. "I hate facts, don't you?" she said. "They say so little." And instantly she launched into a rambling, compelling description of her new "nounless novel," which will take her "away from the 'I.' It will have no nouns, only relationships. For a rock that is coming to hit you is very different from a rock that is lying peacefully in a river-bed. And if you don't name the thing, you can't seize it." She told me that in the Hopi language you express yourself solely with the verb and that Einstein said that one could not express relativity in the American language, but only in Chinese, Japanese, or the American Indian tongues. Then she told me that she was disappointed in women's poetry, that she was unable to understand how women could still say, "the sun rises," in all good faith.

As that moment, Adelaide Bean came in to announce that our time was absolutely over, and, with a flurry of warm hugs and kisses, and promises to meet again in a hole in the ground or in a hollow tree somewhere, before I had time to plead for just a few last facts, I found myself out in the street, my eyes blinking from the bright daylight.

The day before Meridel Le Sueur left New York City, however, I did call her at Adelaide Bean's house to ask her to tell me the facts of her life. "Write to me, and I'll send them to you," she said cheerfully. I did.

A few weeks later I received a wonderfully impressionistic rapid rundown of factual details, typed on the backs of two mimeographed subscription forms from West End Press requesting fifteen dollar charter memberships "to keep in print the works of Meridel Le Sueur and other writers who cry out against an unjust and oppressive society," the leaflets were plastered with quotes like "The poor disappeared, Reagan said, in California without a sound," and "They put a hood over the head of Albert Parsons before hanging him and inside the hood he cried Let the Voice of the People be Heard. . . ." and "In Spain a dying regiment wrote Neruda's words in their own Blood."

"This is a history of facts," the letter read, "if your editor doesn't consider them facts then he doesn't know what a fact is. editors rarely do . . .

Born in 1900, the year of the first signed monopoly of james hill and morgan claiming the american earth as their province for eternity and all their heirs forever . . .

Beginning of the most bloody century in history.

I was born with my right arm out in a fist, had to be pushed back, was depressed by what I encountered.

I was born on indian iowa land which once had been so rich, thirteen feet down of pure humus . . .

My father—an itinerant preacher. We wandered from illinois to texas and then started back north. I lived in Oklahoma before it was a state, then kansas and back up to minnesota . . . I was in Minnesota during the war where you were tarred and feathered if you were against it. Our books were burned in the front yard in st. paul. The Non Partisan league a third party made north dakota a socialist state for one year and we were there.

The war was a terrible experience. I was at the trials of those persecuted because they were against the war . . . I was arrested on the steps of the minn-capital for being against the war . . . I was at the anarchist trials and the trials of the liberation mag editors for obstructing the draft . . . Also of Bill Haywood in 1918 Every young man of my age I knew never came back from europe . . . I was in the Palmer raids.

From the twenties to the depression I was trying to make a living in hollywood as stunt woman with pearl white in the Perils of Pauline . . .

I joined the people in the depression, the Workers alliance the unemployed councils from which the girl was written . . .

The writers congress of 1935 . . . the spanish civil war . . . we sent a hundred to the abraham lincoln brigade from Minnesota.

Then the second world war . . . Then the reaction to that war expressed in the Smith and McCarren acts of repression . . . the Korean War, the death of the rosenbergs and the death of, my mother.

I was sent underground in the mccarthy period couldn't get a job my mail opened . . . I couldn't teach or make a living.

My books were sold under the counter if at all . . . I was unpublished . . .

Some date had a child in 1928 and another in 1929

Now have seven grandchildren and thirteen great grandchildren This is a fact . . . everything is a fact . . .

I almost couldn't find the letter. It was folded up inside a book that Meridel Le Sueur had sent me as a gift. I almost didn't realize that anything was written on the backs of the fliers on which she had detailed her life history. But it is a letter that I will treasure forever.

Shortly before I met Meridel Le Sueur, a poet from Texas had given me a magazine of works collected during a series

of women's workshops, outdoor art events, and happenings.
Since Meridel Le Sueur had been a guest during the "research," a working prose version of her "Ballad of the Sow"
appears in the magazine. I had just finished reading three or
four books of Meridel Le Sueur's strike stories when I first
began to read the "Ballad," and I remember being confused
and disappointed at first, feeling that Meridel Le Sueur had
somehow been polluted by the new wave and was no longer
herself. I was genuinely bothered by the discordancy of images I could not seem to assimilate. For, buried in the mine
cave underneath the earth, the more goddess-like images I
associate with the modern feminist movement didn't work
for me. They seem almost contrived, as did the specific
references to female genitalia, female fluids, menstrual
blood, mucous, and milk. And, involuntarily, I sought the
old familiar passage of the men in the mine shafts, lost,
suffering, longed for. I didn't like the use of the old familiar
bible songs intermingled with the calls to the mother. It
seemed to have none of the poetry of Meridel Le Sueur's
early use of song. And the rough language, when it came,
was almost too rough. It felt like a violation.

Yet, disappointed as I thought I was, there was something wondrous about it all. And I read on. Then at the point
in the story when a folktale of a flying sow enters the narrative, I noticed that something strange was happening to me. I
was beginning to be won over. I was beginning to believe. I
was riveted. What had happened?

As I read on, the songs ascended, the rough language
coarsened, and the mixture of beauty and brutality rose to an
almost feverish pitch, the images of eating and being eaten,
of the life fluids emerging from the deadly blackness of the
cruel devouring pits, and of the pig babies, unformed, wide,
gaping mouths, pink worms, who, if they were too many for
the tits, would be cared for by being eaten along with their
dead grandmamas and grandpapas. And then at last the

prose turned into poetry, staying in the poetic shape, until, no longer rent with images of dark pit shafts or the familiar bible songs, but born out of darkness looking for light, it turned into its own song, the "Song For My Time," which Meridel Le Sueur prophesied in the naming of one of her earliest books, and the circle, the cycle somehow became complete.

KATHLEEN RAINE

I *was on the top deck of a double-decker bus, traveling the*
road to Paultons Square between South Kensington
and Chelsea, when I reread Kathleen Raine's "Northumbrian Sequence" for the final time before meeting her. I was
going to visit the woman thought by many to be among the
greatest living English poets and was feeling rather awed by
the fact that she had agreed to see me. I had spent the last
few days immersed in rereading all of her works, her eight
volumes of poetry and three volumes of autobiography, the
last of which had just come out. I took the "tubes" to many
far-off London bookstores trying to locate her two-volume
study, *Blake and Tradition,* which was published in this country by Princeton University Press.

As I would ride the tubes from place to place, reading
about her life or reciting the lines that I remembered from
her poetry, I felt I held her words as in a spell, that they held
me, each tree in them, each bird or bone, becoming a spirit
presence both mythic and magnificent, until I felt that all I
actually saw took on her colors and cadences. Never before

had I met the color red with such intensity, with all its flow of birth and rose and fire of epiphany, its bleeding. It made all of the reds upon London chimney tops much brighter than they would have been.

But mostly I was moved by Kathleen Raine's religiosity. I had been raised an atheist and taught that only human beings could manufacture brightness out of the all-surrounding void. But the radiance that Kathleen Raine evoked with her words came from a place with a reality which I could almost feel.

I was rereading her "Northumbrian Sequence," the section about "Let(ting) in the night" in which the "nameless formless power" embodied in the wind, the rain, and all the Northern ghosts of death, of "unfulfilled desire" come to the poet asking entry. I was trying to fix in my mind its ever-shifting yet relentlessly pounding refrain: "Let in the wind/Let in the rain/Let in the moons tonight/ . . . Let in the snows that numb the grave,/Let in the acorn tree,/The mountain stream and mountain stone,/Let in the bitter sea . . . ," when suddenly—I could almost pinpoint the exact moment—the words and images which had been linking up into a larger whole began to turn into a blur. I could no longer follow my own lines of thinking. I had completely lost my understanding of her metaphysics. However, as I continued to read, it seemed a spirit came from the page to fill my being from a sphere far different from that of the word-formed images which called it up.

Later, when we were together, I tried to describe the nature of my experience to her. I told her how through repeated rereading her poetry had broken through the barriers of my whole atheistic past and brought me to a place where I could come in contact with the powers she has faith in. Then she began to talk about the Cabala. She talked about it for a long, long time. She explained how in Cabalistic tradition there are four graduating realms. First there is the "world of quantity" where perception occurs only on a horizontal level. This is the world that most people operate upon, especially in our contemporary society so obsessed with the materialistic values she deplores. Then there was the "world of the individual soul or psyche from which art images are made." But through art it was occasionally possible to "draw down light" from one of those higher spheres of existence we cannot directly reach, the region of the spirit and the realm of the divine above, "about which, of course, we know nothing."

I told her how it was the search for height I felt most strongly in her poetry, in her cries for a mystical oneness with nature lost to humankind with the coming of language, in her love poems and evocations of the animal spirit which dwells within us all and gives to us our passion. From *Stone and Flower,* her earliest volume of poetry published in 1943 (A bird sings on a matin tree/'Once such a bird was I.'/ . . . Seas, trees and voices cry/'Nature is your nature.'/I reply/'I am what is not what I was . . .") to the just-published thin blue tome, *The Oval Portrait* ("A woman old/I have been so many selves that I am none,/No longer anyone . . . aged with the wisdom of the years./The unbeginning and unending theme/Whose teller and whole tale I am"), her poems brought to me a deep communion with the outward forms in which the intangible life energies reside.

In two old-fashioned armchairs we sat and talked by the warm fire she made in my honor, having heard that all Americans find England cold. We were surrounded by her books, her family mementos, and her English art collection. Upon her walls hung paintings by Ben and Winifred Nicholson, by Collins and David Jones, and three Palmer engravings, two from Milton and the third from Blake's *Book of Job.* There was also a landscape of the western coast of Ireland by the Irish writer and visionary, A.E. There was an air of deep-sought peace about the room, but I knew that it emanated from the woman I was with and not from any of the objects which had marked her journey.

A month or so earlier, Mayotte Magnus had come to photograph her for an exhibition of important British women in the National Portrait Gallery. "Most people's homes reveal their inner lives," Mayotte had told me. "But with Kathleen Raine I knew that her apartment was irrelevant to whom she really was. I took her out into the garden right away."

Among the throngs of famous English women, pictured in the elaborate settings they created through their works and personalities, only Kathleen Raine is shown without a single man-made object. White-haired and wise looking, she gazes from the gallery wall with mystical serenity. The major portion of the "portrait" is dominated by the patterns of the sunlit plants and leaves she draws her inspiration from. She herself occupied only a tiny portion of the photograph, a small space in the lower left-hand corner. But I will never forget her glow.

Now seventy-three, living alone in Paultons Square where she has lived for many years, Kathleen Raine had an unmistakable air of dignity and peace about her. With her I felt the radiance of one who had passed through the trials of her earthly life into a state of spiritual calm which I had rarely seen. There seemed to be no loneliness about her, no great sense of turmoil, although the stories that she told me about her earlier suffering were quite intense. Now, in retrospect, she is able to view the once confusing pattern of her past as the attempted fulfillment of our universal mission to "bear witness" through our individual experience and her particular "task" of retelling what she has seen and lived in poetry.

Although she is far from proud of many of the ways in which she handled incidents in her own life, she recently decided to publish her autobiography. With a characteristic compassion, she refused to release the major portion of the material while her parents were still alive, for "I did not want them to know how much I had suffered. . . . My own children," she added somewhat sadly, "have inherited all of my capacity for suffering without the ability to make it into poetry."

One by one, the three volumes of her autobiography, *Farewell Happy Fields, The Land Unknown,* and *The Lion's Mouth* have come quietly to this country, published by George Braziller, but they have not received the notice they justly deserve. Because of the enormity of aspiration contained in their pages, contrasted against the sorrow that her actual life so often held, they become elegies of hope for all of us and give us the courage to try to live fully even if we must risk getting hurt.

"Most people are afraid to live fully," she said to me, "because living means suffering. To begin to live is to accept the possibility of suffering but also meaning. Unless you are willing to commit yourself to a certain level of consciousness, you can never receive life on a more significant level. But once you do, there is no limit in height. We can go as high as we like."

Kathleen Raine was born in Ilford in 1908. But the formative years of her childhood were spent in Bavington in the far north of England, a land where spoken language was linked to the things and forces it described. "Poetry was not then words on the page, but birds in the air, in the dusk, against the wind . . . it was trees, it was stones and springs, an ever-changing face of things which communicated knowledge words can only remotely capture or evoke."

She early learned the magical significance of corbie, hawk, and heron, birds whose very names meant forces which could not be translated into other words. As part of her Presbyterian education she learned "to know godly from ungodly flowers . . . to put tiger lilies in the church vases I did not need Blake's Tyger to remind me was unthinkable. Not only was a combination (a 'clash' not a harmony) of black and orange manifestly ungodly, but the form of the flowers, with the tense recurve of the petals, the long filaments, too delicately extended, and hung with their heavy-loaded antlers, spoke of nature's unconsecrated mysteries. There was something in so intrinsically perfect a form, besides, to arouse the intelligence, and by so doing ruffle the surface of the glassy sea of calm devotion. Poppies verged on wickedness even as a garden flower."

The feeling that ideas and objects were not separate entities was one that never left her. Nothing could exist without having a deeper meaning. But words were often a barrier to real experiencing. All of her poetry and even academic research into Neoplatonism was merely an effort to reestablish the so much more vivid primal relationship with living she had known when she was young.

She told me about a recent meeting she had with one of the village head-men of the Hopis. "We spoke the same language," she said, "because we lived in the same kind of universe. For both of us earth was the home of the gods, a place where the mere existence of something was inseparable from its meaning." She told me how when Yeats's widow offered her a book of his, she asked instead for an anemone pulsatilla which she had noticed growing in the garden, "the flower at which Thel, in Blake's title page, looks so thoughtfully as she considers mutability. . . . It seemed to me fitting that so Neoplatonic a flower should be growing in Mrs. Yeats's garden: so she gave me the flower, and I pressed it carefully. . . . Blake too must have loved the real flower and not the mere emblem."

From her Scottish mother, Kathleen Raine took all of her love of poetry, her fascination for the wistful and the wild. She took her mother's sense of being an exile from the more beautiful land north of the Border deep into her heart, creat-

ing her own poems of attempted crossings, attempted returns. "My mother was an inspiration," she told me. "My
whole life has been the living out of her unwritten poetry."
She spoke of the place within us all that "we remember and
know but have forgotten," a place which "is either a memory
of a lost state of being or a measure of something as yet
unrealized. From that state of being we are all exiles." Before
I left she gave me the childhood volume of her autobiography, *Farewell Happy Fields*. I shall never forget the story in it
of her infant craving to visit the Wild Hills o'Wannie, a tale
which seems to tell it all.

Here is a portion of the tale:

> . . . before I ever saw that place, "the Wild Hills
> o'Wannie," a line perhaps from some poem by a
> local bard, spoken by my Aunty Peggy Black in her
> sweet treble, was a summons to that other
> world. . . . It was the phrase itself which acted on me
> as a spell . . . The phrase named those hills as a
> place not in the world so much as in the poem;
> promised in the very place the wilderness-in-itself
> of all hills. I had only to reach the Wannies to be in
> that essential world.
>
> So it was that at last, one day, one fair northern
> summer's day, we set out, my mother, my Aunty
> Peggy and my infant self in my little push-car. . . .
> We came to a little crag where in the warren there
> were always a few black rabbits among the brown—
> I knew the place well later. Wild it seemed, without
> wall or man-made road, the creatures wild in the
> rocks, and far and wide. Was this "the Wild Hills
> o'Wannie"? No, I was told, farther on, could I not
> see them in the distance?

They never did reach the wild hills the child had built so
many fantasies about. Apparently the

promises had all been a ruse to keep a baby happy on a walk across those long Northumbrian pastures. . . . They promised that I should go there someday—that beautiful horizon of time. . . . They thought I would forget as soon as they themselves, my purpose to go to that place; but I was, on that day, not the baby in the push-car, but the self I was later to become, or already was. At last poetry came to my aid, and I fell into a chant, repeating the magic phrase over and over until the words become a sort of mantra. "I want to go to the Wild Hills o'Wannie." By incantation I tried to bring near the far bright beauty of the hills. In need of magic for so specific an end I discovered the use of poetry.

Most children lose their early craving for the heights and wilds, their memory of the more perfect place towards which we go, but for the poet, the pathfinder, this longing for the lost paradise only grows more intense with age. As time elapses, and the sense of exile deepens, the loss of even the dream of reaching the wild hills of the imagination in reality must be compensated by the creation of such an inner place through art. Thus Kathleen Raine reached with the word, the only tool she knew, to the more perfect time before the word, creating through that process a language which transcends its function and turns into form. Here is a part of her poem "Exile."

> Then, I had no doubt
> That snowdrops, violets, all creatures, I myself
> Were lovely, were loved, were love.
> Look, they said.
> And I had only to look deep into the heart.
> Dark, deep into the violet, and there read,
> Before I knew of any word for flower or love,
> The flower, the love, the word.

They never wearied of telling their being; and I
Asked of the rose, only more rose, the violet
More violet . . .

I see them now across a void
Wilder and deeper than time and space.
All that I have come to be
Lies between my heart and the rose. . . .

Sometimes from far away
They sign to me;
A violet smiles from the dim verge of darkness,
A raindrop hangs beckoning on the eaves.
And once, in long wet grass,
A young bird looked at me.
Their being is lovely, is love;
And if my love could cross the desert self
That lies between all that I am and all that is,
They would forgive and bless.

Kathleen Raine, separated by intellectual learning from
all her soul once knew, could no longer go backwards to the
time before the word, to the time before

the mind, curious to pursue
Long followed them, as they withdrew
Deep within their inner distances,
Pulled the petals from flowers, the wings from flies,
Hunted the heart with a dissecting-knife
And scattered under a lens the dust of life

Her college years were lonely ones from a spiritual point of
view. Coming to Girton, one of the Cambridge women's
colleges, during an era dominated by "Russell's new logical
positivism, Bloomsbury humanism . . . and the materialist
science of the Cavendish laboratory," she tried to exorcise
from her experience the connections art and magic once had.
"All was of a piece, the new taste and criticism invented to

justify it. There I discovered that the beauties I had hitherto
found in Milton and the romantics were not of the imagination, but imaginary; it was I who had failed to understand
that where I had thought I had seen beauty, there was none. I
and my simple kind had not the courage to retort that, if this
be so, there is more value in the illusion than the reality; still
less than to have seen beauty, to have been moved by feeling, is a fact which cannot be argued away."

Banished from the world of poetry by the rationalist overlay imposed upon it, she turned to botany and zoology to
find the thing that she had lost. "There, among flasks and
retorts, plant tissues and microscopes and the bones of verte-
brates I could still slip off my brave new persona and bathe
in nature's healing stream. The marvels of the universe were
there open to me and I contemplated in awe and delight the
Book of Nature. I could think my own thoughts, arising
unbroken from my childhood's world of the Northumbrian
moors, and perhaps from still deeper ground. As an anonymous student of natural sciences I was more of a poet than
ever among the Cambridge poets. There my experience was
at once aesthetic and magical; those life cycles and transformations, embryology and morphology, that condensation of
force into form."

Because learning had played such an important part in
Kathleen Raine's development, she sought to find new ways
of synthesizing intellectual study and the spirit forces
that so many of the scholars of her time were fighting.
Disillusioned by the Cambridge intellectuals, she sought
out the companionship of mystical thinkers and religious
visionaries. As she would have wanted the child's non-
verbal connection to all living things that her own growing
had deprived her of, she also regretted being unable to par-
take in the religious systems which offered their adherents
the deep connection to the living god she sought. The East-
ern religions, she told me, have always held a special

attraction for her. But although she was highly educated about them, she felt that Western Europeans were excluded from true participation because of the dissimilarity of their roots. The Jewish tradition also has fascinated her, especially lately, because in it "one is born into a total relationship with God; the Jewish God of Life is not theoretical." But it never seemed to be a real option. For a while, under the influence of Graham Greene and her close friend Antonia White, she attempted to become a Catholic. But finally she decided she had to find her meaning in the solitary poet's way.

Through her work on Blake, begun at a time of deep despair, she discovered "the roots of a tradition of excluded knowledge" she was truly part of. This was the Western esoteric and Neoplatonic tradition followed also by Yeats who saw what he described as "the rise of the soul against reason now beginning in the world." In her autobiography she describes how her sense of restless searching was gradually quieted as Blake became her "Virgil and (her) guide; I took the end of his golden string, and began, with an exhilarating sense of return to duty, to wind it into a ball." Even now she speaks about the balance her scholarship gives to her life, "providing an intermediary level between poetry and apathy."

From the beginning Kathleen Raine was drawn in deeply to all situations of sorrow and suffering. In the first volume of her autobiography, she describes the slaughter of the village bull who had "lived his solitary life, marked out from the herd by the brass ring in his nose, and the heavy wrinkled folds of his head and neck" who was sentenced to ritual murder for unknowingly maiming a farmer.

There is no other creature on an English farm who has the power of death in his horns . . . he was the evil-one of our world. Yet by us children the bull's *mana,* his magical animal power was recognized; he was the power of us; no human being in our world had such greatness as his. Theriomorphic gods are older than human, and children, like archaic man, recognize with immediacy the quality of animal-souls. . . . The human world has passed judgment on the animal; the evil beast must yet again be slaughtered. Behind the immediate crime—lay who knows what remote echo of archaic man's profound self condemnation of his own animal nature. . . .

There was a long waiting; the butcher, alone, crossing the yard, gun in hand; a muffled bellow; and as in a Greek tragedy the king is shot behind the heavy doors of the palace, so we waited for the shot, and knew that the great one of our small world, the creature of power, had once again been slaughtered; the strong by the weak, the great by the small.

Only Kathleen Raine, the child that she then was, seemed to comprehend the depths of the murder of mystery beyond the realm of human control.

I saw his pepper-and-salt purplish-brown hide with a sense of infinite compassion: I *was* him. My body suffered in itself the death of the beast, my skin mourning for his skin, my veins, my five senses for his; and when from his anus slipped a mass of faeces, I was ashamed for the abasement of his death.

Embodied in the bull, with his unbridled sexual potency, are all of the miracles of creation and destruction. Kathleen Raine told me that she felt that "most people could play with evil because they never really experienced it." But for her the passion of nature is a manifestation of the power of the living god. Here is a part of her "Cattle Dream," from her first book of poems entitled *Stone and Flower*.

Through the cow's red and wandering eyes
the living elements I view,
I see the blood, I see the iris,
the rainbow band of earthly hue.

From me the gelded cattle run
with muted hooves and tails upright.
In the morning slaughtered and calm
their bones my broth, their flesh my meat. . . .

If in their fury they should kill
and stamp me down with fossil tread
by dawn I should be calm and dead—
deity is reversible

And here is "Tiger's Dream," from the same collection.

On the lawn of green
consecrate to man and wife,
alone but not unseen
the tiger awaits the knife.

Wakefully walking he came,
the eater of men by right,
to the man-eating cannibals home
when dreaming he passes the night.

Oh envy the happy few
whose beds are prepared in the stars.
By the way that spirits know
through the blood of the tiger they pass.

Through the blood of the tiger they pass
to the lawn of greenest green.
Oh envy the happyfew
that dream the tiger's dream.

It would have been impossible for Kathleen Raine to
explore the mysterious passions of nature as intensely as she
does without a firsthand knowledge of the more fiery por-

tions of human nature. The autobiographies are rich with the interplay between the life of the vunerable inner person fully aroused to her own nature and the spiritual death which occurred during those times when the most vital portions of her being were asleep.

"Being a poet is being committed to the truth," she told me. "I have always been distracted from truthfulness by trying to do what I ought." She described her two brief marriages as acts dishonest to her deeper self, as promises given when her "daimon," her living soul, was dead. "If the sexual instinct was that time my undoing," she wrote in retrospect, "it was not through its strength but through its weakness. . . . The sexual instinct is, when awake, and living, vital, bringing together" the people who are meant to meet. In *The Land Unknown,* she describes sexual passion as the closest manifestation of the living god that we can know on a physical level.

From the time Kathleen Raine awakened to the passion locked within her, causing her to flee the numbness that allowed her marriages, she has traveled essentially alone, as perhaps every poet must. In leaving her marriage with Charles Madge, a fellow poet and the father of her children, for a purely carnal love affair, idealized and impossible, she knew that she was following her own pattern in the same way that the trees and plants she wrote about must follow theirs. Now, as she looks back upon the suffering her actions caused the others close to her, it is the promises she would wish to undo rather than the later breakings of them which were essential to set her free.

Throughout literary history we see the effect of "great loves" upon our male poets, as, at different periods of their lives, individual women become their inspiration and their "muse," the object of all of their creative imagining. But although undoubtedly this "muse" relationship existed in some slightly altered form with the majority of our female writers, rarely have they shared the details of its meaning with their readers. Perhaps this is because personal experience in love for a woman is usually relegated to the realms of daily life and need, not compatible with artistic aspiration. Perhaps it is also because of the discomfort of exposing the existence of a passion in which a man becomes merely the vehicle for the important openings of self from which great works of art can grow.

Each of the volumes of Kathleen Raine's autobiography contains its own "great love." And each of the three loves explored is representative of a different stage in the passage towards self-realization.

In *Farewell Happy Fields,* the childhood volume, it is Roland Haye, her father's former student, who provides for her the cultural nurturing she craves, who breaks through her emotional virginity and teaches her to love. Set against the background of long Sunday afternoons listening to the music of Chopin or reading the great (and not so great) romantic poets, the adolescent Kathleen Raine seeks to fuse her soul with that of a man who opened her to all the wonders that she had not previously known. Because of the candidness and philosophic depth with which she writes, we are able to see clearly how the quality of the infatuation comes more from the accelerations in spiritual growth, the shared intellectual pursuits of the young couple than from a love for the particular man. We see how she is drawn not so much to Roland Haye's adoration as to the widening of her own realm of possibility which he seemed empowered to bring about. Her father's cutting short this scarcely realized romance constitutes not merely the breaking of a single isolated involvement but the shattering of the whole form of idealized first love in its pure state.

For many years Kathleen Raine fled from her feelings, protecting herself from the possibility of being deeply hurt by her marriages to men who did not move her. When finally her passion surfaced again, it was directed to a man who evoked all that her artistic self most needed. It was not Alastair, the man, she loved, but the intensity of the desire that he conjured up (perhaps more in his absence than his presence), "an incandescent state in which we look deep into certain aspects of being. . . . The whole structure of nature which as a child I had innocently lived, as a student intellectually contemplated, now revealed itself to me burning with an interior light and glory, awe inspiring. This state, known to all lovers, glorifies every blade of grass with a sacramental quality of holiness." Clearly Kathleen Raine had to know this state to write the poetry that she was meant to write. Although her love affair with Alastair was unworkable as a lasting relationship in the real world, it lent her poetry an aura of intensity which was never to leave it.

But perhaps the most beautiful love story of all occurs in volume three, *The Lion's Mouth,* the tale of her fated meeting with Gavin Maxwell. Because Maxwell was a homosexual, their love remained unrealized in the carnal sense, giving the spiritual and emotional components far more vividness than they would normally have taken on. Here, through the very lack of actualization intrinsic to the relationship, we are given a rare glimpse of how intense the act of being in love can be.

"The powers sent the relationship," she said to me. "On a spiritual level one is always met. On an emotional level we [encounter more difficulty]. If I had been true to myself as a poet and not tried to give in lower human ways" perhaps the outcome would not have been so terrible.

Gavin Maxwell appeared to come to her out of the longed-for past. His childhood was spent near to her, though at the time they had been strangers. After their first encounter they both dreamed the same waking dream about a bird sitting among the upper branches of a rowan tree, only in Kathleen Raine's vision there had been a boy-child sleeping at its feet. They were convinced that they were kindred souls.

Kathleen Raine spent long periods of solitude in Gavin Maxwell's Scottish Highland cottage, writing some of her most moving poetry. Often, in his absence, she would care for Mij, his pet otter and most important companion about whom he wrote his novel, *A Ring of Bright Water*. She was happy there. But one day when an earlier emptiness descended and a cloud came over their strange union, she let the otter escape and he was killed. Ruthlessly she tells the story of mutual vengeance and sorrow that followed, her curse of wrath beneath the old beloved rowan tree that Maxwell claimed bewitched his later life.

Rarely have I met anyone so harsh in self-judgment. I tried to convey to her my enormous admiration for her passion and compassion which so few can reach, and for her striving for perfection which has caused her so much pain, but she dismissed all of my praise.

"Perfectionists can be cruel to other people," she said to me, "destroying their vital illusions. Artists should not destroy other people's structures." She compared her life to the lives of other poets who had wrought great personal suffering on those around them and wondered if her work could justify the pain it caused.

Who will take away
Carry away sorrow,
Bear away grief?

Stream wash away
Float away sorrow.
Flow away, bear away
Wear away sorrow,
Carry away grief . . .

Black crow tear away
Rend away sorrow,

Talon and beak
Pluck out the heart
And the nerves of pain,
Tear away grief . . .

Song sigh away
Breathe away sorrow,
Words tell away,
Spell away sorrow,
Charm away grief.

After Gavin Maxwell's death, Kathleen Raine wrote the
poems in her seventh volume, *On a Deserted Shore*. It is at
once an ode to the impermanence of nature, a song of
mourning for perfection's inevitable decay when it is
touched by earth, and a reaching out towards an order beyond nature where the immortal essence of love remains
permanent.

I cannot weep
Who, when I turn to you in thought
Behold a mystery so deep,
A world upheld upon a breath
That comes in life and goes in death
Troubling dark leaves upon a starry bough.
Who dreams our lives I do not know,
Nor in what land it is we meet.
Memory: beyond recall
The linnet's song,
The clover-scented air;
Yet we were there . . .

Despair—we approach but never reach
That quiet place.
The suicidal leap
Invokes a mercy earth denies:
It is hope

That wakes to anguish
And will not let us sleep . . .

Suddenly the trees looked strangely beautiful:
'It has taken the form of trees,' I said,
'And I of a woman standing by a burn.'
So near I stood to your new state
I saw for a moment as you might
These sheltering boughs of spirit in its flight.
Shall you and I, in all the journeyings of soul,
Remember the rowan tree, the waterfall?

As I sat with Kathleen Raine by her warm fireside, I tried
to find the words to say that from the sorrow in her work the
vision of a greater hope had grown for me than any I had
known before. I left for her my youthful novel on old age,
with all its suicidal anguish and its angers at the world which
must by its essence betray so many of our dreams. But
already I felt the starting of an aging process in which peace
and illumination might triumph.

On the airplane ride home from England I read *The Oval
Portrait,* her most recent book of poetry.

Afternoon sunlight plays
Through trailing leaves I cannot see,
Stirred by a little wind that mixes light and leaf
To filter their quiet pattern on my floor.
Not real, Plato said, the shadowy dancers,
Imponderable
Somewhere beyond, the light; but I am old,
Content with these shadows that visit me,
Present unsummoned, gone without stir.

So angels it may be.

Later she would write to me about how old age is not half
so dark as youth might think. "You'll see," she said in her
last letter, "we don't age with the body. The Neoplatonists

say that as body ages soul grows younger; and in youth the soul is bowed down and stifled by the body and its demands! The second half of life is for the soul."

And I would read again her poem

"No old age, only sorrow"
A woman said; all things new
But I. No shadow
The gods cast,
But I my past.

And I would start to think with happiness about the future.

DAVID GASCOYNE

*I*t was *Kathleen Raine who sent me to visit David Gascoyne:*
"Most of the people I would send you to see are dead," she said to me, "but David is a beautiful man and one of the few real poets left." She spoke of great belief in him, although he has not written for many years. A few days later, I sat in a tidy second-story bedroom on the Isle of Wight, reading Kathleen Raine's essay on David Gascoyne, which his wife, Judy, had brought me along with their family's ritual "breakfast in bed." Published ten years ago in *The Sewanee Review,* the essay ends: "David Gascoyne, under that 'strain which no human mind can stand,' has, like Hölderlin (whom he had written about when he was young), endured for many years the 'quasi-dereliction' of the oracle deserted by the gods who at times possessed him. He has been silent for more than a decade; but, not yet fifty, he may perhaps write again. . . . Whatever the significance of the silence of this poet, the poems he has written are among the few of our

times that bear such eloquent witness to that Truth for which they speak."

Another ten years have passed since these words were written, and still the man, who in his teens was an internationally noticed prodigy, in the forefront of the surrealist movement in the Paris of the thirties and mass observation in England across the Channel, does not speak. Born in 1916, David Gascoyne published his first novel and a book of poems when he was sixteen and used the proceeds to travel to France to work with the surrealists there. His journal from that period has just come out in England, published by Alan Clodd who, despite Gascoyne's long silence has remained entirely faithful to his work. The story of the financial and artistic struggle of a terribly sensitive young man in the frenzied climate of the years right before the Second World War, it is rich in personal impressions of all the prominent figures of the era, among them Pierre-Jean Jouve, Tzara, Auden, Valéry, André Breton, and the Durrells, who were close friends, interweaving melancholy brooding over the meanings of life and art with childishly refreshing anecdotes, reminding us how young he really was. For example, he came to know Cocteau when he brought a sick friend to see *Les Parents Terribles* "wearing simply a fur-coat over his pyjamas and clutching a decanter of brandy, two glasses, and a large silver cigarette-box." When they were rudely turned out of the theater, they demanded to see the author himself. "Cocteau received us with, at first, puzzled surprise, and then, after a moment, with a most charming understanding. 'Mais naturellement', he assured us, 'la pièce était écrite pour être vue en pyjama!' "

By the age of twenty, David Gascoyne had published the only serious English presentation of surrealist theory, a second book of poetry, and several books of translation. His name early became widely known, as he made rapid shifts out of surrealism into a major work on Hölderlin and the German romantics and then once again into Charles

Madge's mass observation movement in London, during the late thirties. When the Spanish Civil War broke out, he went to Barcelona where he told the news in moving poetry over the radio. His journal from that period has just turned up again. By the fifties, he was living once again in France, writing dramatic works. He even wrote a small public affairs pamphlet on Thomas Carlyle, in which he uses Carlyle's views as an underlay for his own writings about "Man among the dark Satanic mills of industrialism [having] lost his Soul, [and] modern society no longer bound together by the cement of living faith, human life, devoid of Spirit, [being] only death and sordid nightmare."

Night Thoughts, a poem for radio in many voices, commissioned in 1955 by the BBC, was his last major work. Now he lives a protected life in a small unpretentious house in Cowes on the Isle of Wight, midway between the two countries where his most productive years were spent. His new wife, Judy Lewis Gascoyne, a woman of most amazing philanthropic energy currently engaged in a theater-arts project to help young people learn to speak, gave me a detailed description of his schedule as soon as I stepped off the boat.

"David likes things to be very regular," she said. "He will come down today at a quarter to four, when we will all take tea. It is the hour that he usually comes down. And I hope you will not be offended if he watches television at night. It means a great deal to him. He likes visitors, but he does not like to have the order of things changed. And on Sunday mornings, we always stay in bed until noon. I will bring your breakfast up to you after I have fixed David's. On Sunday afternoon, if you can stay, David and I go to read poetry over the air to be broadcast to all the hospitals throughout the Isle of Wight."

Expectantly I settled down with Judy in their cozy little living room to listen to her stories of the poet she had recently come to know and marry. It was after his mother died, and he was feeling great despair, recuperating from a breakdown, that the two met. He was a patient in the hospital where she was working. One day she was reading poetry to the patients. She warned them that a certain poem by David Gascoyne would be difficult and at first refused to listen to the man who cried from the far bed insistently, "But I am David Gascoyne," as patients in mental distress so often will cry they are Caesar or Mary or Christ. But eventually he was able to convince her of the truth of his identity, whereupon she took him home and slowly nursed him back to health. Thus the woman who kept house for the Beatles and Bob Dylan during the famous Isle of Wight music festivals, who offered "hot tubs" to campers, filling their laps with literature all about her latest philanthropic causes while they soaked, now cares for David Gascoyne in every conceivable way.

Slowly my lap filled up with the poet's books, articles all about him and carefully collected scrapbooks which Judy was showering upon me, talking proudly. The whole atmosphere emanated "home" in every sense of the word. It emanated family, comfort, and deep security. Pictures of Judy's smiling grandchildren were hanging everywhere, and standing on the mantelpiece, on bureaus, cabinets, and chests of drawers.

At exactly a quarter to four, a poet himself arrived. I was immediately struck by his stature. His handsome face was troubled and his body filled the doorway where he stood. With a majestic stiffness he moved toward his arm-chair by the fire and haltingly sat down. I remember him as a giant, although now, in retrospect, I am unsure how much of this impression was based upon the physical reality and how much upon some other more spiritual quality that emanated from him. Lawrence Durrell, in his introduction to David Gascoyne's journal, repeatedly mentions his subject's "charm and good looks" but never his unusual height. His hand also seemed very large as it moved awkwardly across

the frontispieces of the books I brought him to sign. There
was a massive power in its partially arrested motion, an
unarticulated eloquence in its rheumatic stance.

At first I was extremely uneasy. The silence of the poet
was taking on a deep and terrifying symbolism I could not
quite fathom. I asked many questions, in an attempt to dilute
the heaviness with which the atmosphere was filled. Thus I
found out about the French surrealists he had known when
he was young. "They were very like French revolutionaries," he remarked. "Very puritanical. Artaud," he said,
"was very terrifying to see," and Breton, whom he always
admired, "was too dictatorial." He told me about the time
they shocked him in the range of their irreverence by throw-
ing chairs at the religious funeral of a friend and fellow
surrealist who committed suicide. The person who had influenced him most was the Marxist Catholic poet Pierre-Jean
Jouve, whose wife for a time was his psychoanalyst.

Through an extended tea to an elegant many-course dinner by candlelight, we sat, David patiently answering every
question I asked. He gave detailed descriptions of the interior of Dali's studio and Duchamp's special door constructed
with two doorways so that it could be both closed and
opened at all times. I filled him in on recent facts about some
of the writers from America he knew from long ago, and he
in turn talked of his acquaintance with Djuna Barnes, his
encounter with Carson McCullers, who at the time had a
paralyzed arm, and of the old wooden house where Hart
Crane lived. He had known many people.

But whether it was past or present we were speaking of, I
had the feeling that each memory, image, or story came to
him like a fragmented shard seen through the far end of a
stilled kaleidoscope, irrelevant in every way to the person he
had become. And gradually, although he was quite willing to
cooperate with all my questions, I decided that I would stop
asking them and try to listen to his silence. We all relaxed

somewhat and waited for the evening shows on the BBC to
start.

David, who had been a choirboy at Salisbury when he
was a child, was particularly looking forward to the drama-
tized version of Verdi's *Macbeth* scheduled after the weekly
serial he always watched. I will never forget the moment it
came on. The sun was just finishing its setting outside and
through the window echoed the oranges cast by the fire in
the hearth, while the flame-like background behind the
chorus on the color television set glowed forth from the far
corner in an almost matching hue. The singers had been
choreographed in a silhouetted pattern, cruciform shape, set
off against the simulated flames, as their voices rose up in
pain, while in small stark white type the station superimposed a running literal translation of the poetry they sang.

There was a stillness in the room as we were watching.
David's face was drawn and his attention was riveted. Judy,
who had been working hard all day attending him, slept in
an armchair with her feet up high. Her eyes were closed
serenely and her head uplifted, making her appear trans-
fixed. And while the fire, sun outside, and television back-
drop grew even more luminous against the night sky's dark
and the black crucifix of singers on the screen, the white
worded caption below it blazed:

The oppression is upon us. The homeland is
forsaken.

It seemed to say it all for all of us, for David, the song
from which it came more powerful than any poem could be.
And yet I knew that from the power of such song had come
his greatest poetry.

And as I watched the caption flickering upon the screen, I
seemed to hear again the echoed words of his last major
poem, more than twenty years removed but still alive with
its apocalyptic quality.

Let those who hear our voices, be aware
That Night now reigns on earth. Nocturnal listeners,
The time you hear me in is one of darkness,
And round us, as within us, battle rages

The choral voices, raised in Latin singing that I could not understand, began to evoke for me the tone of David's final poem of prophecy before he had grown still with awe. In 1955, his words had been the ones that people had heard on the BBC, as many voices rose in the dramatic recitation of *Night Thoughts*. It was his London that had come alive. I felt the power of his words:

At night I've often walked on the Embankment of the
    Thames
And seen the Power Station's brick cliffs dominate the
    scene
Over on the South Bank, and its twin pairs of giant stacks
Outpouring over London their perpetual offering
Of smoke in heavy swags fit for a sacrifical rite
Propitiating some brute Carthaginian deity:
And thought they stood like symbols for the worship of
    our age:
The pillars of a temple raised to man-made Power and
    Light.

Here in a moment of blazing luminosity, his violated city had become both the symbolic witness and the silent "spokes-vehicle" for the desecration of the power which, if mankind is to survive, must be turned again to light. Born out of the mass observation movement's aim to make poetry political, using quite literally "the handwriting on the walls" (graffiti, newpaper headlines, advertisements, and other remnants of mass culture) in the way the surrealists had juxtaposed irreconcilable elements to create a new transcendent whole, this poem becomes a kind of ultimate realization of that movement's purposes. As it draws towards its final stanzas, a lone voice rises up out of the solitude:

> I stand here speaking of my nothingness; and yet I am a
>   man.
> It is my heart that speaks, abasing itself in dread before
> that colossal inscrutability; overwhelmed by the total
>   evidence
> that what is there must be. I cannot understand how ever I
>   am
> able to address what faces me, and yet I know I somehow
>   must
> respond. From out of that profound night-blue abyss of
>   starry
> vacancy comes the command: 'Lift up your heart! . . .' I
>   raise
> my spellbound head and face to face with what I cannot
>   name
> I worship and adore. . . .
> I think I somehow thus may be absolved of the whole
> failure to be truly man. I am a man. I cry out of my
> darkness. I could not cry if I were in complete despair. . . .
>
> Now the man who spoke aloud just now out of his dark
>   into the
> darkness: (to no one? to someone? the mystery is not
>   mine to
> solve that each must face alone) the man who had said: 'I
>   could
> not cry if I were in despair,' turns presently towards the
> lighted windows. . . . And as he goes, begins to realize that
> something has changed in him. . . . Silence had delivered
>   its
> essential message to him, and he had responded. Now he
>   feels

that he no longer has the need to reassure himself with words.

When I asked David why he no longer wrote, he answered quite simply that he had nothing else to say and felt that poetry should say something. He clearly did not want to probe the matter further. I said, "Do you think you spent it all doing so very much when you were young?" He said, "Perhaps."

With great fervor and verve, he had entered the literary world, all worlds. Rapidly he had devoured philosophic systems of thought, artistic and political movements, leaving each one as he became dissatisfied and moving on. By the time he turned sixteen his book of poetry, *Roman Balcony and Other Poems* and his novel, *Opening Day* had already been published, their meager proceeds paying his passage to France. It seemed that nothing stopped him in those days, as he earned his keep, literally from week to week, taking on odd translation jobs and other literary work his friends would try to find for him. We see something of his reckless and soaring spirit in the opening lines of his second book of poetry, *Man's Life Is This Meat.*

At sound of heaven cracking, stars collide
From trembling atmosphere such forms condense
As Earth has never gazed upon before:
A chariot with horses, wheels immense,
The hills declare a prodigy, amazed

Melodramatic, and probably embarrassing to the mature poet, for David Gascoyne later omitted them from both anthologies of his collected works, they give a clue to the enormous energy of striving which allowed him to produce works of such a profound nature when he was so young.

In the introduction to David Gascoyne's *Paris Journal*

(1938–39), Lawrence Durrell wrote how "there was never a moment of doubt as to his vocation," describing his "extraordinary maturity" and his "productive despair" which "made him a sort of Rimbaud of precocity." What caused the enormous productivity of David Gascoyne's early years, and what so suddenly stripped it away? There is a definite relationship in the journal between the frequent waves of suicidal depression evoked by a discomfort in the world of cosmic nature and the sense of mission to survive to utter the "great cry." During the periods of political activity or close work with artistic movements, when the madness seemed to come more from without, his sensitivity found productive channels and perhaps some slight alleviation. But at other times the level at which he experienced, saw, and felt totally overwhelmed him.

When I asked Kathleen Raine why David suffered more than most people, she told me about an angel a shoemaker in a Tolstoy short story found, who never could become acclimated to life on this earth. "David is pure poet," she said. "He is a finely tuned instrument that cannot be adjusted to conditions of this world."

As a choirboy, he was exposed to beauty and transcendence early. But the world that he was asked to prove his manhood in was full of dissonance and hate. He joined the surrealists in trying to make art out of the ugliness that he could not escape, all the while longing for an earlier more universal beauty he once knew. Here is a journal entry from his surrealist period, written after a concert in which Bach's "St. Matthew Passion" had been sung.

> The lovely chorales I know so well because we used often to sing them at Salisbury, brought a lump into my throat and made me long to be able to sing them again. The lofty, shadowy-roofed nave, the calm iridescence of the distant candles, the voices

climbing upwards amid the obscurity of the pillars, brought back a luminous recollection of everything that was most beautiful in the days when I was at the choir-school and wore an Eton suit and a white frill— days which now seem to belong to another life.

Bach's greatness in this work lies in his extraordinary power of transforming the great pain and sorrow of the rejection, betrayal, flagellation, crucifixion, and entombment of Christ, into an unearthly calm and sweetness; of transfiguring grief and suffering into the radiance of a peaceful sky. This is the operation of the greatest art: resolution of the most violent contradictions, creation of harmony out of opposites—elevation, consolation.

The David Gascoyne who wrote those words had been hard hit by the failure of life to measure up to the standards of beauty that he knew in art. But he was bravely trying to reconcile the two. Surrealist thinking, with its focus upon recombining irreconcilable elements into radiant new configurations held an important attraction for him. In it he saw the possibility of changing ugliness to art and giving the powerful inner states he felt, his waking dreams and nightmares, some external validation. His *Short Survey of Surrealism* begins:

Confined from early childhood in a world that almost everything . . . will tell him is the one and only *real* world and that, as almost no one, on the contrary, will point to him, is a prison, man— l'homme moyen sensuel—bound hand and foot . . . is forever barred except in sleep from that other plane of existence where stones fall upwards and the sun shines by night, if it chooses, and where even the trees talk freely with the statues that have come down forever from their pedestals—a world to which the entrance has generally been supposed, up till now, to be the sole privilege of poets and other madmen. For it is undeniably true that the oneiric domain is still regarded in very much the same way as was the erotic domain during the Victorian era, that the dream is useless, as escape from reality, the dreamer a self-indulgent lazy person, is the accepted view of an overwhelming majority. How, then, can man reconcile himself to the fact that he spends more than a third of his life on earth in sleep, and that he spends the whole time of his sleeping in a world that his conscious mind despises.

Unable to escape from his intrinsic intensity and super-sensitivity to all stimuli (external and internal alike) he tried in every way he could to give it a validity and purpose. He tried to bridge the gap between his world and that of others, seeking through surrealism a reclamation of the "lyrical element," which formerly belonged only to poets and madmen, for the masses. But also he was asking for an initiation into violence, irrationality, and unpredictability. He was asking for a system of thought to help him cope with the bitter brutality of life and make a meaning out of it. By meeting ugliness head on, he made a real attempt to exorcise its power to annihilate his hopes. Here is a poem from that period entitled "Putrified Disgust."

Beyond that savage pretence of knowledge
Beyond that posture of oblivious dream
Into the divided terrain of anguish
Where one walks with bound hands
Where one walks with knotted hair
With eyes searching the zenith. . . .

How could we touch that carrion?
A sudden spasm saves us
A pure disgust illumines us

The music of the spheres is silent
Our hands lie still upon the counterpane
And the herds come home.

He tried over and over to meet the violence and despair of
life with energetic lust. In his poem to Dali we feel that he
was practically daring himself to look unabashed at everything that brought him horror.

The face of the precipice is black with lovers;
The sun above them is a bag of nails; the spring's
First rivers hide among their hair,
Goliath plunges his hand into the poisoned well
And bows his head and feels my feet walk through his
        brain. . . .
The smooth plain with its mirrors listens to the cliff
Like a basilisk eating flowers.
And the children, lost in the shadows of the catacombs,
Call to the mirrors for help. . . .
A flock of banners fight their way through the
        telescoped forest
And fly away like birds towards the sound of roasting
        meat.
Sand falls into the boiling rivers through the telescopes
        mouth
And forms clear drops of acid with petals of whirling
        flame.
Heraldic animals wade through the asphyxia of
        planets,
Butterflies burst from their skins and grow long
        tongues like plants,
The plants play games with a suit of mail like a cloud.
Mirrors write Goliath's name upon my forehead,
While the children are killed in the smoke of the
        catacombs
And lovers float down from the cliffs like rain.

When David Gascoyne wrote in his journal of the con-
flicting substances that he was made of, ice and fire, he chose
to honor his fiery side. His attempts to take on the cold
distance of the surrealist paintings his poetry often described
were ultimately unsuccessful. And, although he wrote elo-
quently in his *Survey of Surrealism* of Dali's three great images—"excrement, blood and putrefaction"—as potential
vehicles for the forbidden and desired states, in his poems
about these artists what we feel most strongly is his pain.
We feel a madness coming in his soul that will not let him
sleep. Here is his poem to Yves Tanguy:

> The worlds are breaking in my head
> Blown by the brainless wind
> That comes from afar
> Swollen with dusk and dust
> And hysterical rain
>
> The fading cries of the light
> Awaken the endless desert
> Engrossed in its tropical slumber
> Enclosed by the dead grey oceans
> Enclasped by the arms of the night
>
> The worlds are breaking in my head
> Their fragments are crumbs of despair
> The food of the solitary damned
> Who await the gross tumult of turbulent
> Days bringing change without end.
>
> The worlds are breaking in my head
> The fuming future sleeps no more
> For their seeds are beginning to grow
> To creep and to cry midst the
> Rocks of the deserts to come
>
> Planetary seed
> Sown by the grotesque wind
> Whose head is so swollen with rumours

Whose hands are so urgent with tumours
Whose feet are so deep in the sand.

In a world gone mad, the dividing line between the visionary and the madman is a tenuous one. Because David Gascoyne was so sensitive to the disharmony both within his being and all around it, he sought in every way he could to discover the epiphanies which such disharmony might hold. In his surrealism book he wrote about the possibility of making the magical experiences of madmen and poets available to everyone. Was he also asking, in turn, to have the comfort of living peacefully in the world extended to himself? Later, as he moved away from the surrealists into a study of the eighteenth century German romantic poet, Hölderlin (with whom he identified closely), he would elevate madness itself. "Knowledge accompanied by damnation, the transcendental vision whose cost is madness. The romantic movement, with which opened the capitalist epoch now drawing to its cataclysmic finale, seems like a voice proclaiming the historical command: 'Thou shalt go thus far, but no further!'

Will the future show the birth of a race who will have superseded this decree?"

Speaking of Hölderlin he says, "We find the whole adventure of the romantics epitomized in its profoundest sense: he carried within himself the germ of the development and the resolution of its contradiction. He was one of the most thoroughgoing of romantics, because he went mad, and madness is the logical development of romanticism; and he went beyond romanticism, because his poetry is stronger than despair, and reaches into the future and the light."

If one could justify madness, it would be possible to balance the very precarious scale which fluctuates between despair and hope, between the darkness and desire for the sun. Movingly, David Gascoyne describes himself also

when he writes of the German "poets and philosophers of
nostalgia and the night. A disturbed night whose paths lead
far among forgotten things, mysterious dreams and madness.
And yet a night that precedes the dawn, and is full of longing
for the sun."

It is the endless night, whose every star
Is in the spirit like the snow of dawn,
Whose meteors are the brilliance of summer,
And whose wind and rain
Are all the halycon freshness of the valley rivers,
Where the swans,
White, white in the light of dreams,
Still dip their heads.

Clear night!
He has no need of candles who can see
A longer, more celestial day than ours.

In following Hölderlin downward, David Gascoyne descended into a metaphysical darkness so deep that his angry
atheism and his doubt became the source of a new apocalyptic and religious light. As the world plunged towards the
darkness of the Nazi age, his probing of the void took on a
tone of almost desperate prophecy and longing for the
murdered Christianity. Here is the poem "Tenebrae" which
begins the requiem-like series he entitles "Miserere."

'It is finished.' The last nail
Has consummated the inhuman pattern, and the veil
Is torn. God's wounds are numbered.
All is now withdrawn: void yawns
The rock-hewn tomb. There is no more
Regeneration in the stricken sun,
The hope of faith no more,
No height no depth no sign
And no more history.

Thus may it be: and worse.
And may we know Thy perfect darkness.
And may we into hell descend with Thee.

And here is the last part of "De Profundis," two poems later, still comparatively early in the journey down.

Because the depths
Are clear with only death's
Marsh-light, because the rock of grief
Is clearly too extreme for us to breach:
Deepen our depths,
And aid our unbelief.

In his journal David Gascoyne had written about the need to utter the great cry. He wrote:

> The Chinese towns are blazing, the Foreign Office is disquieted by the report that still further detachments of Italian troops are being exported into ruined Spain, British warships are being torpedoed in the Mediterranean, the mounted police charge into crowds of demonstrators at another Mosley march through London—and yet out of the very monotony of world-violence, a sort of lull has fallen, a last or penultimate breathing space before the grand-finale (which will perhaps never take place?).
> And all over Europe and America, unknown and silent, engrossed in painful solitude . . . there are still living men from whom escape, from time to time, a few clusters of phrases dictated by a frantic and obscure compulsion. . . . And ("horribles travaillaies") are perhaps preparing something like a great cry that must go up from the heart of our time. . . .
> After having been ill and terribly depressed and without money to eat for several days, I looked in

the mirror and saw an ugly sunken face, and suddenly thought: I might die this winter. And I wanted
to cry out to something for strength, but there was
nothing *outside* I could pray to: there was only the
thought of the depth *inside,* where the instincts are
constantly struggling—the hidden force of the
blood, with which it is possible, for those who know
how, to make a sort of contact, and so suppress the
death which threatens momentarily to obtain a
dominating hold over the centre of the *moi,*—Jouve
calls the hidden force "le cerf sanglant." I wanted to
call out: *Cerf!* give me strength never to succumb
before I have uttered the great cry!

As David Gascoyne's focus shifts from trying to make an
art by which to reconcile himself to all of the world's horrible inequities and contradictions to uttering aloud the cry to
change them, his voice turns more clear and strong. He
finally gathers the courage to let in the full impact of his
despair so that his anger turning outward can begin to shat-
ter the destructiveness of life that caused it. And, at last, the
personal and cosmic coalesce towards a new universality. In
anger breaking through to hope, he asks in "Kyrie"

Is man's destructive lust insatiable? There is
Grief in the blow that shatters the innocent face.
Pain blots out clearer sense. And pleasure suffers
The trial thrust of death in even the bride's embrace.

The black catastrophe that can lay waste our worlds
May be unconsciously desired. Fear masks our face;
And tears as warm and cruelly wrung as blood
Are tumbling even in the mouth of our grimace.

How can our hope ring true? Fatality of guilt
And complicated anguish confounds time and place;

While from the tottering ancestral house an angry
   voice
Resounds in prophecy. Grant us extraordinary grace,

Oh spirit hidden in the dark in us and deep,
And bring to light the dream out of our sleep.

He calls upon the murdered Christ

Whose is this horrifying face,
This putrid flesh, discoloured, flayed,
Fed on by flies, scorched by the sun?
Whose are these hollow red-filmed eyes
And thorn-spiked head and spear-stuck side? . . .

and through him tells all of mankind

The turning point of history
Must come. Yet the complacent and the proud
And who exploit and kill, may be denied—
Christ of Revolution and of Poetry—
The resurrection and the life
Wrought by your spirit's blood. . . .

Not from a monstrance silver-wrought
But from the tree of human pain
Redeem our sterile misery,
Christ of Revolution and of Poetry,
That man's long journey through the night
May not have been in vain.

Interestingly, the coming of the Second World War,
which lent an affirmation in external reality to David Gascoyne's inner anguish, gave him the validation that he
needed to pursue his work of entering misery to overcome it.
In his journal he describes the "deadly spiritual sickness" of
his contemporaries which

express(es) itself chiefly in the form of that intellectual sophistication and detachment which betrays a

latent *fundamental indifference to everything.* . . . It has seemed to me that this malady of my contemporaries is most likely to be cured by their having to undergo some immediate experience of what I call Anguish (sense of the Void; of being personally implicated in imminent human disaster and in tragic human futility, etc.) . . . that this is a necessary and salutary experience, through which the thinking minority on whom the whole future of society depends may be purged of their false and sterile intellectual *detachment.* . . . I believe that we must learn to *think with our hearts* and to *feel with our minds;* and that we shall be forced to learn this lesson by the ultimately inescapable Anguish brought by the War.

The last entry of his *Paris Journal* is dated October 10, 1939. After that he passes for a time out of his personal anguish to the universal pain he voices in his final and perhaps most lasting poetry. This final journal entry reads:

–My 23rd birthday. Sixth week of the War.
–*Vita Nuova.* In spite of the War (probably in fact, *because* of it), I have truly emerged at last from the dark, constricting chrysalis of the last few years of my life and now *I am.* Everything—inner and outer, and the whole relationship between them—is now clear. I have accepted the great fundamental contradiction, and have died of it; and am risen again; and now the old Contradiction is no more. It now remains to me to write down my total vision. . . .

And here (for the time being, at any rate), I close this journal. It has served its purpose. The most profound of the many intuitions I have recorded in it have all come *"true".* The ploughing and the sowing have borne harvest. My life has passed on to another plane.

I am full of a great wonder and astonishment,

and of exaltation. The world is very deep, the War is horrifying; yet the Future of this Century has begun to burn with an extraordinary, unseen and secret radiance, which I feel I can no longer speak of here, since it has become my task to proclaim it to those to whom it has not yet appeared. . . .

May I be granted the grace not to fail or become discouraged before the purpose and responsibility of a new life.

Thirty-eight years later we sat together in a silence neither one of us could break. The nuclear holocaust of Hiroshima, the wars in Korea, Vietnam, and the Middle East, had come between the David Gascoyne who once wrote those words and the man that I met. Generations had been born that remained shocked and silent, that tried hard to fight against the world's inequities and, failing, had sunk deep into a state of apathy again.

So much to tell: so measurelessly more
Than this poor rusting pen could ever dare
To try to scratch a hint of. . . . Words are marks
That flicker through men's minds like quick black dust;
That falling, finally obliterate the faint
Glow their speech emanates. Too soon all sparks

Of vivid meaning are extinguished by
The saturated wadding of Man's tongue. . . .
And yet, I lie, I lie:
Can even Omega discount
The startling miracle of human song?

The War brought in its wake sorrows too difficult to bear. Among those murdered by the Nazis was a young Dane called Bent whose relationship with David Gascoyne "was the nearest approach to [his] particular conception of love

[he] ever experienced." Shortly after the onset of the affair, David Gascoyne wrote:

> Now Bent has proved to me that one's dreams *can* come true, I shall never again be able to put *only* a black mark against existence. . . . Always on the edge of life, in the margin just over the border, like money and love, lie beauty's undistorted forms and colours, and the eternal delight of energy, and the music that we long to hear. And in a purity of light we never see on this side of confusion, the real embodiment of all the images we give to our desires: golden flesh, the smell of hair, the tenderness of unfamiliar hands, moist warmth and gentle pain between the thighs, and eyes almost as near to eyes as mouth to mouth and full of disturbed depths and shadows;—movements of strength and grace, slimness and smooth resistance of a defiant, pliant body discovered in its final secrecy.

The loss of Bent, the wars, the sufferings he saw, were blows from which he did not easily recover. His periods of breakdown, common in so many people with a keener vision, stand as statements of the horror of our world, set dark against the light he tried to shed. His silence had not developed in a vacuum, I knew, but was a real response, as deep as anything he ever wrote.

From the moment I arrived, I noticed the persistence with which he checked his watch. For constantly, regardless of the subject of the conversation, his eyes flitted from its small round face up to the larger circle that the clock above the mantel made, and then, studiously back down to the watch. At first I thought he was trying to make the time pass faster to eliminate my presence. Then, later, I began to wonder if he was awaiting anxiously the starting of the evening programming on the BBC. But the night shows had come and gone, another day begun, and still he fixated upon the clock hands, until finally I said to him, "What is it that you would like the time to do? Would you like to go backwards or forwards?"

"So you have noticed my obsession with the time," he said, smiling reluctantly. "I do not want it to do anything. I just would like it to be always right."

But later when I related this incident to Kathleen Raine, she quickly reassured me he wanted "time to turn into eternity."

CHARLOTTE WOLFF

I *walked into Charlotte Wolff's lecture about her newly* published book, *Bisexuality: A Study,* half by accident. Generally I am resistant to attempts to give a scientific overlay to a subject so intensely personal as human passion. Perhaps also I was resistant to the whole idea of bisexuality, which by its very definition, allows for a simultaneity of love involvements, diluting the age-old impassioned one-to-one relationship, which, for all its residue of trauma, seems still to form the basis for the things I love best about our literature, our way of life, and art.

I arrived quite late at the London Ethical Society where the lecture was being held. There was a record crowd and only standing room was left in the ornate wood-paneled meeting hall filled up with white-haired men. There were mostly doctors, scientists, and scholars in the audience, appearing to be left over from another century. It was as if they had been called to life out of an aquatint of the Vienna days when psychoanalysis was born. Later on in the month Charlotte Wolff would lecture at Sappho, the lesbian society

which was so helpful in her research, talking informally with the young women who attend their socials in the smoke-filled upstairs chamber of a back-street pub, but this first presentation of her carefully collected information was solemn and scholarly. Even the smattering of young students attending seemed lifted from an era long since gone.

However the content of the evening certainly was not. For here, through extensive historical background, synthesis of past psychological writings, personal reactions, lengthy interviews, and statistical data, Charlotte Wolff was challenging the very idea of fixed sexual identity upon which so much of the structure of society is based. There had recently been many forward-reaching books on homosexuality (her own earlier study, *Love Between Women,* among them) but, because they dealt with specifically delineated special-interest groups, the unaffected "normal" majority could freely choose to disregard their revelations about larger human issues. Now, through stating that we are *all* bisexual, however we express it, Charlotte Wolff was speaking to this other audience as well, and asking for their meaningful involvement in the re-evaluation of those stereotyped sexual roles which have crippled the full capacity of every human being, spiritual, emotional, and sensual.

Through the bisexual, whom she sees acting out the many sides of human possibility the rest of us have fled from, Charlotte Wolff was beginning to sow the seeds for a more universal revolution in our attitudes. She had written

> Society has categorized people according to their sexual orientation, and has never understood that there is only *human sexuality* with manifold expressions. . . . Bisexuals and homosexuals, on the other hand, make valiant efforts to free themselves from the fetters of its conditioning power. . . . By reason of their rebellion, they are inclined to reject second-

hand living as laid down by social conventions. It is not surprising that one finds many of them in the forefront of the fight for a new society, a society where authenticity is the guiding principle . . . they are, by virtue of their still precarious position, well endowed to realize that the assignment of roles which rules every aspect of behaviour, permeates society like an infectious disease, that there is a social sickness about that leads via hypocrisy and falsity to alienation. Their own fringe position makes them particularly sensitive to the schizoid shortcomings of our society where nobody knows what the other thinks or feels, and where relationships lose their essential qualities—solidity and trust. Needless to say, it is not the privilege of bisexual and homosexual people alone to be aware of this predicament, but their particular make-up encourages a greater flexibility of approach towards new ventures, because they have less to lose and are less afraid of change. Only in a bisexual society can human beings get rid of the sexual compartments in which they are entrenched, and understand that we are all in the same boat, only in different attire.

In her lecture Charlotte Wolff was speaking of how the men and women in her study, although physically drawn to both sexes, almost all experienced their strongest emotional attachments with women. Through personal anecdotes many of the men in the audience confirmed this, telling stories of how women were beginning to turn away and redirect their energies and nurturance towards one another, given the "permission" by the women's movement. Due to the present structure of the family, all human beings experience their primal and most influential ties with women. Would we all return to women if allowed? In self-protection, heterosexual

society had built a system of rigid defenses against the actualization of this possibility, giving men most of the power
over our collective destiny, but there were many destructive
ramifications. Interestingly, in Charlotte Wolff's study,
those bisexuals who were more physically compelled by
men were often victims of early violent sexual enounters
with aggressive males. There were many instances of rape
during childhood or adolescence among the women, many
instances of early homosexual assault among the men. What
would happen if society prohibited the subtle forms of rape
through which the strong maintain their territory, exacting a
nurturance not freely given in exchange for financial security, social standing, and physical protection?

In America, unknown to Charlotte Wolff, a woman called
Dorothy Dinnerstein was beginning to attract attention for a
scholarly book calling for a serious reevaluation of our current gender roles. She was proposing a new way of child-
rearing in which the father would equally share in the nurturing role. By way of explanation of her title, *The Mermaid
and the Minotaur: Sexual Arrangements and Human Malaise,* she
had written: "The treacherous mermaid, seductive and im-
penetrable female representative of the dark and magic un-
derwater world from which our life comes and in which we
cannot live, lures voyagers to their doom. The fearsome
minotaur, gigantic and eternally infantile offspring of a
mother's unnatural lust, male representative of mindless,
greedy power, insatiably devours live human flesh." With a
strong focus upon ecology, Dorothy Dinnerstein was asking
us as "self-creating animals" to shift our preconceived ideas
of gender which are threatening the very survival of the
species, for she stated "until we grow strong enough to
renounce the pernicious prevailing forms of collaboration
between the sexes, both man and woman will remain semi-
human, monstrous."

I had just finished reading Dorothy Dinnerstein's book

before I came to England. Now, far across the ocean, separated by enormous differences in background and approach, Charlotte Wolff was seated behind a cumbersome wood desk defying the very notions of "masculinity" and "femininity" which form the basis for even our most progressive explorations of androgyny. I was immediately captivated by her aura. It was that of neither man nor woman, but rather of a sage whose physical aspect had begun to embody all of the unlived-out sides of humankind. There was a special radiance about her face, a universal quality about her deeply shadowed smile which turned it into every smile beneath her darting dark black eyes. Her brow was very definite and deep. Her shock of sideswept hair was very black. She reminded me of Doctor Matthew O'Connor from Djuna Barnes's *Nightwood,* one of her favorite books, not so much in her looks, but in a certain emanation that she bore of having seen the night yet surfaced, of having been chosen by fate to be the listener to the tales of passion no one else would hear.

In striking contrast to the stark black turtleneck she wore were her expressive long, white hands, lending a silent rhythmic undertow of added meaning to the words she spoke. Later I learned that she was famous for her pioneering studies of the human hand. She had started as a poet. Among the French surrealists, her innovative scientific work interpreting hand shapes and gestures earned her a special place in the affections of André Breton, Paul Éluard, Antoine de St. Exupery, and others in their circle. Later again she emigrated to England where she spent several years studying the hands of monkeys and apes in the London zoo, helped by her friends Aldous and Maria Huxley through whom she met most of the foremost literary figures of the day, Virginia Woolf, T.S. Eliot, and Thomas Mann, as well as Lady Ottoline [Morrell], the hostess of the great salons, whom she saw as one of the most lonely women she had ever encountered.

Like Lady Ottoline, Charlotte Wolff led a glittering exterior life, but in her inner world, described quite poignantly in her autobiography, *On The Way to Myself,* she was very alone, an exile haunted by a nostalgia for a sense of belonging that could never be complete. Born near Danzig, a city with a history of uncertain nationality, she belonged to the last generation of German Jews to take part in that highly educated legendary old world childhood which Hitler was soon to destroy forever. Her autobiography is rich with the descriptions of a life-style where poetry, art, and learning still were held in reverence, a universe in which each book, each building passed, and every work of art embodied many layerings of great historic memories. Although my own connection with the German Jews is rather distant, my European roots having been severed several generations before I was born, through my German refugee stepmother I felt I knew already the long solitary afternoons of study depicted so vividly by Charlotte Wolff, as well as the meandering traditional walks which seemed to take on a ritualistic importance in the absorption of a culture now irreparably stolen from us. I felt I too could share her sense of exile from the beauties of a way of life our people would never experience again.

Nostalgia, like a lilting melody, runs through the pages of all of her books, be they scientific, poetic, or autobiographical, her own irreparable sense of exile becoming the catalyzing force for the envisioning of a world where all categorizations of people will be rendered meaningless and all human beings will have a place. I will never forget the way she compares the lesbian in modern society to the wandering Jew, a perpetual outsider fired by romanticism and great dreams, the way in which the fantasies of reunion with the mother and creation of a new and nurturing "motherland" are joined. Even her early study, *A Psychology of Gesture,* begins with the dream of how we can all be united if only we

can begin to shed the "emotional masks" which we hide our
true intensity behind.

> Inhibited expression is comparable to a river
> blocked by a dam; it floods the surrounding country
> and seeks numerous more or less torturous outlets.
> When direct expression is barred the inner dynamism
> discovers other outlets, less obvious and more
> bizarre.

She tells the story of the tower of Babel, illustrating

> how the peoples of the earth became divided and
> alienated through the spoken word. . . . But however
> far apart in colour, habits, manners, and religion
> people may be, the universal language of gesture can
> forge links between them. For gesture-language is
> practically the same in all human beings, and it fol-
> lows that it must correspond to the primary level of
> existence. . . . Man without movement is "dead" and
> the vital concern of each individual is to find adequate
> expression for his inner dynamism.

Several decades later she would extend her ideas about
increasing our creative powers and our joy of life through
unleashing those bodily movements which come from the
regions of our deepest emotions into the whole of human
sexuality. But now, looking back, it does not seem coinci-
dental that the hand, symbolic in its very essence of potential
reaching out, was what began her work. Nor does it appear
accidental that it was through focusing upon my hands that
she first "met" me as a person.

We were strangers to each other when I first went to see
her. She had read only one article of mine, and I had heard
her speak just once, upon the occasion of the London Ethical
Society meeting. So naturally, although I had just had a
harrowing time with a writer intent upon challenging my

every word and was feeling uncomfortable, tired and cold, I
kept our conversation appropriately impersonal.

By way of intellectual interest, I started to describe the
other writer's way of constructing her craft out of a constant
violent challenge to our destructive complacency of thinking.
I was rather impressed with how, through abstract understanding, I was able to transcend my weakness and my hurt.
I did not notice how my hands betrayed me. But of course
Charlotte Wolff did. She showed me how unconsciously I
had tucked them completely inward close upon the region of
my heart, calling my attention to the way in which my wrists
were folded, touching one another, and my fingers tightly
curled, through her detailed description conveying to me the
whole emotional tone of the previous encounter with a startling clarity. Then, abruptly, she stopped her analysis, order-
ing me to sit absolutely still in silence while she left the
room. A few minutes later she returned with a cup of hot
coffee and a luxurious French pastry which she keeps for her
own moments of depletion in a hidden tin.

It was the smallest simplest act of healing, yet now, remembering the overwhelming wonderment of my response,
I wonder if that uncanny ability to "hear" the hungers which
were lurking far beneath the surface was what brought her so
close to all of the artists "in costume" that she writes about,
the lonely soul hiding behind the masks of their created
natures.

Her work on hands had always been her means of entrée
into the world she was most compelled by. From the moment she left Germany and came to Paris, she received an
enthusiastic reception from the artistic and scientific commu-
nities alike. Professor Wallon, an eminent teacher and psychologist, offered her his full support and personal guidance
in her works. The surrealists all flocked to her, won over by
her rather sensational gift of seeing into the deepest recesses
of people by intently staring at their hands. But as her notori-

ety increased, she became conscious of a growing dichotomy
between the superficial glamour of her "gift" and the deeper
meaning of her study which so few could see.

> I became aware . . . of an invisible obstacle, invisi-
> ble to others but not to me. I could not blind myself to
> the fact that I owed popularity and esteem in the
> world of the elect to some sensational appeal which
> left my own Self in suspense, or worse, hidden in a
> corner. The engine of my vitality had to be driven at
> high speed practically all the time, with the result that
> I felt a sense of frustration, of fatigue and depression.
> How differently had my pattern affected me when I
> lived in Germany. . . . As a refugee I had landed on
> the wrong side of the fence, in a marvelous fairy tale
> which could never be my reality. Luckily, I knew this
> and could accept the wonders and experiences of the
> stolen goods bestowed on me.

And yet was not all of life in some way a "stolen" experience? How many of us were as free as she had been in
learning to accept the wonders and to create out of our
personal bereavements? As I sat with this beautiful woman
who had been loved by the German health-workers in the
public clinics where she first practiced medicine, the French
surrealists, British literary luminaries, and lonely salon
women, I thought of the ending of her only novel called *An
Older Love*. I thought of how the narrator, a healer like herself, is forced to watch her own slow fading from the tale she
tells.

> Demoted as a friend, but more than ever fasci-
> nated as an observer, I was in no mood to pay
> attention to gestures of rejection. The time had come
> to play a disingenuous role, and to substitute diplo-
> macy for spontaneity.
> A refugee remains an outsider however well he

may do, a destiny he shares with the artist. And many consider both to be rootless creatures, parasites on society, even when they are instrumental in regenerating it.

The apartment in which I met with Charlotte Wolff was not her home. I never did find out to whom it belonged. It was located in one of those impersonal high-rise apartment buildings which are still refreshingly rare in London. In fact the doorman explained the mechanics of the elevators to me in a way that indicated that he still saw such machines as rather awesome monsters. I remember very little of the interior. Unlike the Ethical Society meeting room, whose ornate old-world aspect remains indelibly engraved inside my mind, no impressions of the flat returned to me, only the vague uncolored imprint of the rectangle that was the sofa where I sat facing her chair, and a recollection that the kitchen from which the tin that held the pastries came was to the right. At one point during our visit someone else came into the apartment, but she disappeared so quickly I could catch only a fleeting glimpse of her.

We spoke a great deal about hands that afternoon, and about the relationship between movement, emotional imagery, and self-expression. We talked about the connection between poetry and science. "For me poetry is blue," she said. "Science is yellow and sex is red. Only a poet is a good scientist."

From childhood on she had hated all labels, all limitations of possibility. She spoke of how the sense of maleness and femaleness was rooted in the self and should be free from society's manipulations. One knew whom one was by an "entirely natural magnetic sensation in the self, a difference in rhythm, allegro, staccato." And one should be open to "love for persons" without category.

She told me about her early work with Julian Huxley, and how she had studied old- and new-world monkeys and apes, as well as the defective and mentally sick. Freely our conversation wandered from hand movements to sexuality and back, the details of both areas of interest merging to form a single tapestry elucidating human personality. She had investigated the hands of thirty boxers and had found that underneath the fists they forced themselves to make lurked very frightened men. She had won the confidence of Ravel, Derain, and Duchamp, although Picasso refused to have anything to do with her. "He told Breton he would not have anybody 'exploring' him, after what Gertrude Stein had written about him."

Virginia Woolf was very skeptical about the validity of "hand reading" at first, but once "the ice was broken" she let Charlotte Wolff examine her palms and the back parts of her hands for more than an hour. Later she invited her to her home in Tavistock Square. Their parting is poignantly described in Charlotte Wolff's autobiography.

> It was a strange adieu. She looked very tall and ethereal in the fading light, when she suddenly stretched out her right arm in a large gesture, saying in a bewildered, low voice: "All these people passing, all these people passing." Indeed, there were many on their way on the pavement and in the square. I have never forgotten the words and the tone of her voice. She uttered them with a meaning only known to herself, but I detected her loneliness and her fear of getting lost. When she waved her hand at me once more, she seemed so far away. I never set eyes on her again.

Nostalgia, like a drumbeat, gives the life-force to her scientific findings and penetrates deep into the pulse of every personal tale she tells, nostalgia, romance, and anxiety. "There is no such thing as original sin," she says, "only original anxiety." She had become a cherished confidant of

Lady Ottoline, enjoying the warmth of her social circle as well as the more intimate weekly visits alone which had become their habit. But once Lady Ottoline had thanked her publicly for a small bunch of violets which she had not brought. It should have been a minor incident, forgotten easily, except that Lady Ottoline had stated that she felt that the selection of the violets seemed symbolic of the perfect understanding the two women had. Overcome with embarrassment, Charlotte Wolff had remained silent, unable to admit that the loving attribution of the gift was a mistake. But from that time on, the memory of the gratitude bestowed in what had been a counterfeit situation began to turn into a torment, the single occasion of an imperfect connection overshadowing the real depth upon which the friendship had been based, until, eventually, Charlotte Wolff fled entirely.

A lover of all that is vibrant, imaginative, and wild, of the illusion and the throbbing pulse of life the artist makes to mitigate the inevitable emptiness, it is her inner dread of lack of authenticity which gives her search for truth its passion and its poetry. Obsessed with partaking in "stolen" recognition and the fear of being found out (emotions operative in all of us), she paints a moving picture of those men and women whose sexuality forces them to wear the masks of what they cannot be.

In the new book about bisexuality we become immersed in the plight of men driven to act out the homosexual part of their natures in sordid public places, often without even seeing the faces of their partners, men for whom the homosexual act is inexorably equated with danger and impersonality. We also come to know transsexuals whose deep-rooted fear of their own homosexual inclinations has led them to undergo complicated surgery in order to conform to the mandates of a heterosexual society. But we are shown not only the distortions and the pains, we see also the courage in taking untrodden paths, the joy of taking stolen pleasures, and the fleeting ecstasies. We see fumbling, striving human beings trying to make their own creative meanings in the nightmare world which we have made.

As I read the passages about the sexual underground, I was reminded of the pages of her autobiography which describe her life as an adolescent medical student, inebriated with the frenzied wild night life of an escapist Berlin in the last stages of inflationary euphoria and pleasure-seeking which preceded its takeover by the Nazis. There she had begun her studies of the human hand, not yet knowing that they would lead to anything important. Spending her days in study at the university and her evenings in the cafés, where the search for erotic and intellectual arousal blended at a constantly escalating level of intensity, she came to know the writer Walter Benjamin, one of her first supporters. She also spent time with Jaeckel, the painter, and the poet Else Lasker-Shuler who, calling herself the "Prince of Thebes," dared to dress as an ancient Egyptian man. "Women smoking cigars received one and dancing went on between girls. At about midnight a kind of gavotte was danced under the direction of a tall woman with an aquiline nose and a somrbrero, mumbling words and orders which were meant to be a sort of Black Magic. We called her Napoleon. . . ." Although it quickly became apparent that the created ecstasy was part of a bravado put on to obscure the coming doom of an entire people, Charlotte Wolff was able to carry away from the experience a consciousness of the capacity of human beings to create their own colors, solutions, and artistic illusions.

Not thinking of her as a fiction writer, I was amazed by the intensity of dramatic development embodied in her novel. While all of her nonfiction is about the need to speak aloud the loves the world will not allow, *An Older Love* is the story of four aging women who cannot. Deeply connected to each other by loves they can neither articulate nor fully realize, they move towards death, trapped in the patterns they refuse to recognize yet elevated through the stirring

depth of their emotions. It is a beautifully written book, rich
in the subtleties of human nature which she knows so well, a
rare merging of psychology and poetry. Bringing together
her earliest involvement with the human hand and her more
recent preoccupation with the field of sexuality, each move,
each gesture and unspoken facial alteration takes on a
weighty significance, drawing us further into the inner lives
of her characters.

> I saw myself looking straight at her, but she re-
> sponded only with sideways glances. I suspected
> that she did the same with her nearest and dearest.
> Shyness made her afraid to look and be looked at.
> Then my imagination pictured her weeding the ve-
> getable garden. Her large, reddish hands pounced
> on the plants like birds of prey. Her thumbs had
> always worried me. They were misshapen, clubbed
> thumbs, to me a sign of bad temper. All of a sudden
> she would make abrupt hand movements, as if she
> were going to slap someone's face. Such notes of
> violence would have frightened me if I had loved
> her.

But perhaps the most moving writing of all occurs in her
scientific study, *Love between Women,* clearly the subject closest to her heart. Here, through numerous small biographical
vignettes and several full length personal histories, we see
emerging the picture of a kind of love, which because it
serves no "practical" function either reproductively or in
terms of social advancement, is ruled entirely by romanticism and emotional desires:—

> [E]motional intimacy means all and everything.
> With an emotional disposition inclined to intensity
> and drama, homosexual women resemble hunters in
> constant pursuit of 'magical' love. . . .

What is the motivation behind this haunting drive towards romantic love, which has the qualities of obsession? Lesbians expect from one another nothing less than the wish-fulfillment of an incestuous mother-daughter relationship. It has to be an all-enveloping union, from which the male is absolutely excluded. Their desire and their search reach out for a goal which is entirely their own. It is essentially different from the longings of heterosexual people and homosexual men. One may ask, why is their love essentially different from any other kind of love? Because the sameness of their psychophysical reactions entails the possibility of an understanding on every level so complete as to be incomparable to any other form of love. There is no need to grope for the right response; it is given per se. Thus lesbian love can, at its best, fulfill the impossible: the intertwining of the most exciting emotional ecstasy with the greatest sensuous intimacy.

The "histories" that follow, so subjective, so intense, and yet so scientific, dispel all of our notions about the need for objective distance in research, for it is the urgency of Charlotte Wolff's personal connection to her subject matter which gives to it its impact. And it is only through the personal that she is able to touch with intimate compassion the more universal strivings of the human soul, so that at last we are left not only with a specific portrait of the lesbian, but with a statement of strength and possibility which touches all of us, whatever our choices in our lives may be, giving us all the courage to try to enact the romantic loves we dream of, to each imagine our own versions of the loves the world will not allow, the taboo "fulfillment of the impossible" from which our meaning and our art is born.

OLGA BROUMAS AND
STANLEY KUNITZ

t was one of those early spring afternoons of premature heat, when twenty-seven-year-old Olga Broumas, born and raised in Greece, received the Yale Younger Poets Prize. Students, faculty, community literary people, and the entire staff of Yale University Press which sponsored the award sat silently on wood and brocade old-world chairs in front of cubicles filled up with books, around the dark wood massive banquet table in the center of the room, or sprawled upon the thick gold carpets of the university press library, while on a low stage, also carpeted in gold and furnished with ornate settees, Olga Broumas stood and "read" her love poems written to women, swaying with her eyes shut tight in a soft wave-like motion that echoed the oceanic rhythm of her words.

I was amazed to see how open the mixed audience was in the reception of these impassioned poems which touch so directly the fluid throbbing spaces deep within the female

body. I was surprised to see how freely this poetic rendering of woman's awakening to powers of the senses long forbidden by this world was accepted, to see how moved the listeners were. But most of all I was affected by the heartfelt introduction by Stanley Kunitz, Pulitzer Prize-winning poet and former poetry consultant for the Library of Congress, who, as editor of the series, had chosen Olga Broumas to receive the prize.

I had come to New Haven somewhat suspicious, wondering what lurked behind the awarding of such a tradition-hallowed honor to a radical lesbian, wondering who was mocking whom. Instead I found a rare and beautiful meeting of two revolutionary spirits. Joined by a love of musicality in language and a belief in the power of poetry to say those vital things which must be said, Broumas and Kunitz share a commitment to art as a catalyst of change which cuts across the barriers of age and sex and time. Stanley Kunitz, a lifelong revolutionary who had his first exposure to injustice in society as a young reporter covering the Sacco-Vanzetti trial, graduated from Harvard *summa cum laude* only to find that he could not become a member of the faculty "because Anglo-Saxons would resent being taught by Jews" (after which he went away to spend the next thirty years of his life isolated on a farm). For him Olga Broumas's poetry is important not only for its linguistic beauty, but because it embodies that "sudden revelation that comes in a moment of revolution, that upsurge of vitality and opportunity to find out who you are."

This is the last year of his eight-year term as editor of the series. During those years he has selected books that touched upon almost every contemporary political and cultural issue while maintaining high standards of artistic and linguistic excellence. Among his choices was Michael Casey's *Obscenities,* the only major book of poems by a single author to come out of the Vietnam War. When he was young, he said, he did not know a single older artist. These "beautiful young people" whom he has helped get started have become part of his family. Some will go very far, he feels, among them Olga Broumas. Others may never write again. But he made it very clear that he was committed to giving the prize to the best manuscript of the year, not to betting upon the future geniuses as if they were horses in a race.

In this era of watered-down collectives, committees, and group decisions in the most personal realms of art, the Yale Younger Poets Series, now in its seventy-fourth year, has remained beholden to honoring the choice of a single judge. "Three will never dare." Stanley Kunitz told me, and since poetry is such "an ambiguous area of taste" the resultant decision of even a small committee will be the lowest common denominator, a safe choice. The Yale series has not only survived, while so many others have fallen by the wayside, but it has given early support to such leading poets as Paul Engle, James Agee, Muriel Rukeyser, William Meredith, Adrienne Rich, W.S. Merwin, James Tate, and Sandra Hochman, perhaps precisely because a system based upon a unilateral responsibility both calls for a total commitment and allows a certain audacity in the final decision.

In Olga Broumas's work Kunitz recognized a quality of transcendence, an ability to move toward epiphanies. He said that he did not believe in words for the sake of words, that poetry must have its roots in human values, and that this was imperative in terms of the quality of civilization and survival of society, that the importance of the arts is to keep in mind what is truly valuable and can restore us. During the first five years of his editorship, he awarded the prize to men. For the last three it has gone to women, "because women are writing the most interesting poetry now." If the prize had not gone to Olga Broumas this year, he said, it would have gone to another woman. He spoke of the sense of life that exudes

from Broumas's poetry, the great vitality, and when I asked
him if he felt at all threatened by her lesbian-separatist position, he answered, "if you stop being vulnerable, you die."

Olga Broumas's poetry is a cry for love between women
on all levels. Vivid with the sensual imagery and rhythms of
her native Greek ocean, reclaimed in the pulsing warm
sources of energy found and acknowledged finally within the
female body, her writing speaks to and for not only those
women who love each other physically, but to and for all
women slowly learning to support and love each other, as
well as ultimately to all humankind trying to evolve new
ways of touching inwardly and of responding.

Lush language here is no mere ornament, nor is the intri-
cacy of the play on sound an artifice. Rather, the sensuous
precision with which each word is made to fit into the other,
the mounting mergings of sound and meaning, become both
the echo and the metaphor for the development of a new
"tongue" of touch, of caring and awakening. For Olga Broumas, for whom English is a second tongue, there is a certain
urgency about the rendering in words those deepest and
most hidden feelings of women, echoing the entry into those
so-long-forbidden spaces in the female body and the heart.
In *Artemis,* the poem from which her title comes, she writes:

> I work
> in silver the tongue-like forms
> that curve around a throat
>
> an arm-pit, the upper
> thigh, whose significance stirs in me
> like a curviform alphabet
> that defies
>
> decoding, appears
> to consist of vowels, beginning with O, the O-
> mega, horseshoe, the cave of sound
> What tiny fragments

survive, mangled into our language
I am a woman committed to
a politics
of transliteration, the methodology

of a mind
stunned at the suddenly
possible shifts of meaning—for which
like amnesiacs

in a ward on fire, we must
find words
or burn

Slowly, not only Olga Broumas, but all women today seeking their inner meanings and their passions and their sound, are crossing first through bastions of rage and anger out of the former numbness and muteness which kept from them the pain embodied in their hidden hopes for understanding and for love. Slowly they are coming to know not only their own strength but their own softness and vulnerability from which the possibility of being profoundly affected by the outer world can come. There is a sense of sacred gentleness with which Olga Broumas forges a new language of sensation, a delicacy in her particular way of opening what has been closed and in the dark so long, which I think is what accounts for the willingness of audiences to travel with her

into that milky landscape, where braille
is a tongue for lovers, where tongue,
fingers, lips
share a lidless eye.

Because, as our culture changes, women are finding more ways to experience joy and fulfillment in their own lives, the angry poetry of the early feminists is giving way to something softer, fuller, and more based on images of affirmation and of life than death and rage. At the dinner following the award ceremony, Stanley Kunitz mentioned that he could not relate to the poems of Anne Sexton, one of the writers Broumas feels most indebted to (among the others are Adrienne Rich, Silvia Plath, Judy Grahn, and Virginia Woolf), because "Anne Sexton screamed," and I realized that Anne Sexton had to scream because she spoke into a void that had no echo for her voice, because there was no way as yet of building in reality on what she had to say. Unlike those older poets who knew so little affirmation in their lives, Olga Broumas will not have to scream so loud, for she knows she is heard, nor will she have to kill herself because she cannot make the life she needs, but she is fully conscious of her debt to the brave women before her who cried out so courageously in the darkness.

Perhaps because Olga Broumas is still so young, and yet so bright, so open and receptive, coming to consciousness in this period of rapid change for women, the shifts from the earlier feminist visions of rage to the emerging ones of hope and joy are clearly visible and all contained within her book, condensed within a relatively short space. She spoke of how when pain is our primary and most intense experience, it must inevitably become the material for our fantasies, for our poetry and our art. For Olga Broumas the awakening from pain came in the form of letting through her love for women.

In "Beauty and the Beast" she writes:

For years I fantasized pain
driving, driving
me over each threshold
I thought I had, till finally
the joy in my flesh would break loose with the terrible
    strain . . .

        Pain the link
to existence: pinch your own tissue, howl
yourself from sleep. But that night was too soon

after passion
had shocked the marrow alive in my hungry bones. The
 boy
fled from my laughter
painfully, and I
leaned and touched, leaned
and touched you, mesmerized, woman, stunned

by the tangible
pleasure that gripped my ribs, every time
like a caged beast, bewildered
by this late, this essential heat.

In her goddess poems, which comprise the first section of
her book, her women are still inaccessible. They are experienced as either cold as stone or dangerous in their devouring
sexual power. Calypso gathers "the women like talismans,
one by one" and uses them, while Circe, wildly flaunting the
sensual beauty that has wounded women throughout time,
turns her seductiveness into a weapon, as she changes men
to "whistling, grunting" swine, and the maenads scream out
in chorus:

Hell has no fury like the fury of women. Scorned
from birth by their mothers who
must deliver the heritage: signs, methods,
artifacts, what-they-remember
intact to them, and who have no time
for sentiment, only warnings. Hell has no fury.

And hell has no fury like fury of women. Scorning
themselves in each other's image
they would deny that image
even to god
as she laughs at them, scornfully
through her cloven maw. Hell has no rage like this
women's rage.

Olga Broumas's Aphrodite, the goddess of man's love and lust, is turned to stone from being made the object for a love which leaves her out. "The one with the stone cups and the stone face . . . with the thighs of marble . . . this idol, stones through her ears . . . so like a stone statue, herself" holds a grinding stone in her lap that should be soft, the symbol of her anger at the stolen nurturance which never was returned.

In Olga Broumas's poetry we see the breaking through of the stone barriers which make us deaf and helpless, mute and angry, as women slowly learn to care for themselves, the first step in truly reaching out towards others. Olga Broumas mentioned that her poetry often precedes her conscious thinking, that it paves the way for where she is trying to go. "Memory piece/for Baby Jane," the first poem Olga Broumas ever wrote to a woman, describes the tender late night bathing of a woman who, to ward off hurt, has made herself both tough and numb. The waters that come over Baby Jane, whose shoulders love her, and whose body, whose own lap, becomes her mother, as she sings to herself at night, are not the cleansing waters sanctifying carnal sin. Rather they are sensuous flowing waters, warm and salty with the force of a woman, embodying the beginnings of caring and comforting. They are as full of life and fluid as the embryonic ocean tides they echo, but what is born of them is not the other but the self.

It is only after this love for the self is solidified that the other truly can be let in, that the soothing salt waters and the "warm pulsing places that wait/that wait" can be shared, allowing pleasure, joy, and softness in. In "Lullabye," one of Olga Broumas's most recent poems, we finally feel this happening.

> . . . You leaned
> into me like a ship embracing
> the waters it was meant to shun, the dangerous

undertow it was meant to float on
and not claim. My love
this love has not been
forbidden. Its one risk: sailing
down through the warm laterals of the heart
to a windless bay. One of our mothers prays for this
    song

to survive
her own deafened ears, the other
pieces together a second quilt, one that will
cover us, not for shame, nor
decency, but

as the chill
streetlights fluoresce on our light sleep, finally
tucking us in, for warmth.

As nurturance, first of the self (in "memory piece/for Baby
Jane) and then of the other (as in "Lullabye"), begins to
replace experiencing the self as an object for the satisfaction
of someone else's needs, Olga Broumas is able to return to
her image of the angry Aphrodite made of stone and clearly
exorcise that hardened part of her own being. In her Cinder-
ella poem, which begins with the Anne Sexton epigraph,
"the joy that isn't shared/I heard, dies young," she is able to
finally and forcefully reject the role that the world regaled
her with, that of the "fortunate" chosen woman on whose
foot the glass slipper of entry fits.

        . . . the lure
of a job, the ruse of a choice, a woman forced
to bear witness, falsely
against my kind

    She is able to say:
        . . . Give
me my ashes. A cold stove, a cinder-block pillow, wet

canvas shoes in my sisters', my sisters' hut. Or I swear
I'll die young
like those favored before me, hand-picked each one
for her joyful heart.

Olga Broumas, extremely beautiful, gifted in every way,
and radiant, stood proudly with Cynthia Orr, her storyteller
lover, surrounded by the heterosexual world that afternoon
in Yale University Press Library. She feels it is essential for
people to know that when women choose each other it is not
because they have no other options, but because in so doing
they are choosing themselves. Olga Broumas, who, because
of her youth, her beauty and success and brilliance, could
have had almost any life, considers her rejection of the Cin-
derella syndrome a political and moral act of the highest
importance.

Although Olga Broumas is not that much younger than
many of the other women writers around, it is as if she has
somehow skipped a step, has passed over with surprisingly
little pain a great deal which has wounded, paralyzed, or
killed so many others. Part of it has to do with being foreign,
she thinks, for it is easier for her to let go of the oppressive
aspects of a culture which has not left its indelible imprints
upon her. Taking what she chooses of her old-world tradi-
tions, the warm water imagery, the deeply layered reso-
nances of its ancient language and its myths, she is able to
start again in our culture and in English, which for her "is
clean and not fraught with old trauma," giving her the opportunity to be quite literally reborn.

PASSAGES

REDISCOVERING
MARY WEBB

*E*very so often one discovers something which strikes a
chord so personal and so sacred that, though it
is unfamiliar, it seems to function as a fragment of a memory
long lost. Such was my feeling when I first came across
Precious Bane, by Mary Webb, the story of the triumph of the
inner spirit of a woman born deformed and thought a witch
by all the mountain people. Written in first person Shropshire dialect, it is simultaneously so simple and so profound
that it shocks the humanness inside of one and sends deep
reverberations through the flesh as the forces of a primitive
and terrifyingly beauteous nature grow personified and large.

Although I wandered all over the city, collecting all the
books by Mary Webb that I could find, I resisted trying to
find out much about who had created the works I loved so
much. There was something appealingly magical in the obscurity which cloaked this writer about whom so few had
heard, whose writings had come to me like the wafting

refrains of a folk song listened to in childhood which I alone
could be affected by.

Yet, much as I wanted to savor my private affection for
Mary Webb (perhaps because the intensity of my attraction
to her was inexplicable, could never form the material for an
intellectual discussion, indeed might even be reduced to
nothingness by analytic penetration), I was angry that others
with writings less rough and more innovative in terms of
plot, with philosophic underlays that went beyond a passion-
ately breathing oneness with nature coupled with an all-too-
Christian sense of good, had gone on to become famous,
while this devoutly sentimental turn-of-the century teller of
tales had been all but lost. Thus the half-wild early works of
Mary Webb, with their amazing anthropomorphically poetic
passages, unabashed musings on the larger meaning of existence, and thorny apocalypses mixed with rustic folk ballads
and mystic lore, became my private hobby, and *Precious Bane*
the birthday gift I brought to all my friends.

It was always a joy to me to make a present of the little
volume which would inevitably be tattered and gray from
decades of sitting unclaimed in used book stores. For I
would know that hidden underneath the frayed exterior the
book was radiant and beautiful within, just like Prue Sarn,
the woman with the hare-shotten lip whose tale illuminates
its pages.

Possibly Mary Webb would have disappeared into an
obscurity far more total, but for the fact that the British prime
minister, the Honorable Stanley Baldwin, fell in love with
Precious Bane which reevoked for him not only the nostalgia
for a more primitive past that it seems to call up in all of us,
but also a specific nostalgia for the land where he grew up.
Shortly before her early death, he wrote to Mary Webb:

> My people lived in Shropshire for centuries be-
> fore they migrated to Worcestershire, and I spent

my earliest years in Bedley, which is on the border.
In your book I seem to hear again the speech and
turns of phrase which surrounded me in the
nursery. . . . Thank you a thousand times for it.

Mary Webb answered full of gratitude that "the man with
the least leisure . . . of anybody in the British Empire should
spare time to write [her] a letter with his own hand" and sent
him a little bunch of violets for his writing table. Seven
months after she died, the prime minister made a speech
about her at the Royal Literary Fund Annual Dinner and the
six books she had written during her life time were reprinted
with introductions by Martin Armstrong, John Buchan,
H.R.L. Sheppard, Robert Lynd, Walter de la Mare, and
Stanley Baldwin himself.
    Because of the intangible sentimental quality of Mary
Webb's special genius, there has been a general reluctance to
acknowledge her as a major writer. Although she is included
in various dictionaries of literary biography, she is given the
"uncertain position of 'regional writer,' " kept down by the
fact that her "plots are contrived" and her characters mere
"mouthpieces" who "betray her least ingratiating quality, a
high strung, blunt didacticism."
    I quote this criticism here only because I feel that it brings
up the very important issue, not only of the relative merit of
Mary Webb's writing, but that of what a novel is meant to
be. In this age of hangover from the Hemingway derived
realism with its dictates of "Show it through the action. Do
not tell it!" and its stern taboos on philosophic passages in
which the author's voice is manifest, these books which ask
over and over the most elemental questions and attempt to
answer them in the elucidation of the meaning of each tree,
each howling wind and mountain to those humans who
dwell in their aura are bound to make the modern reader
uncomfortable. Yet it was in an effort to give voice and

clarity to those most fundamental things that art was first evolved. And it is in Mary Webb's insistent inclusion of all that puzzles her that her real contribution lies, as it is in the intensity of her caring that the people and the elements she writes about are transformed into moving symbols of mythic dimensions.

In *The Golden Arrow,* Mary Webb's first novel, the question which she asks is what will happen if we feel, if we make ourselves available to the enormous and often ruthlessly irrational powers of the natural world and our own inner passions. Because of the magic intertwining of the forces of the universe, the inexorable cleavages, cold winds, and stony edges, the more that feeling is let in, the more suffering will be inevitable. And yet, out of this also grows the ecstasy and the quieter content of oneness with the flow of nature and its haunting beauty, the resurrection. Thus John, the shepherd father (based upon Mary Webb's own father whom she worshipped), at peace with the world through an understanding that embodies an intrinsic atheism overlaid with faith and trust, retells the ancient folktale of the golden arrow to his children as they awaken to adulthood.

In time gone by the lads and wenches in these parts was used to go about Easter and look for the golden arrow. It met be along of them getting sally-blossom for Palm Sunday as the story came. . . . And it was said that if two as were walking out found the arrow they'd cling to it fast though it met wound them sore. And it was said that there'd be a charm on 'em, and sorrow, and a vast of joy. And nought could part 'em, neither in the flower of life nor in the brown winrow. And the tale goes that once long ago two found it in the sally-thickets down yonder. And they came through Slepe singing, and with such a scent of apple-blow about 'em as

never was—though apple-blow time was a full
month off; and such a power of honeybees about 'em
as you only see in summer-time. And they went like
folks that want nought of any man, walking fast and
looking far. And never a soul saw them after.

Those lovers who find the golden arrow will inevitably
be caught in the complicated drama caused by the collision
and attempted fusion of two necessarily separate natures.
The more intensely radiant the meeting, the more given of
each's individual essence to the other, the more difficult will
be the journey towards eventual synthesis and harmony.
And yet in Mary Webb's scheme of things, it is only in this
total journey that eventual fulfillment lies.

Thus, in *The Golden Arrow,* it is with a certain elation
mixed with terror that we watch Deborah risk her own
downfall by enveloping Stephen in a spiritual love so all-
inclusive and so static in its clasp that all that is transient and
fluid in him is compelled to flee. For from the beginning,
there is a certain vibrance about their entry into the union
that, despite the many complications, betokens hope for
something higher.

Had [Stephen] loved Deborah with all his being
they would have been safe. But he loved in the manner of many civilized people, and not in Deborah's
way—for she was primeval, and her realities had
never been sponged away. His had. . . . [however]
she did not know that under his new-found material-
ism lurked a superstition more powerful than hers,
because unplumbed by him. This was partially the
outcome of the dark doctrines he had been taught as a
child; it was partly inherited from a race that had
come of the soil, as Deborah's had; it was also the
primeval instinct of the poet and the savage, who find
in rock and flower a fearful alphabet. He had no idea

that this existed in him, and he had not the conscious poet's safety-valve of expression.

All of Mary Webb's novels, all love stories in their own ways, focus upon that period of initial awakening from animal innocence in which all actions, like those of the natural forces, are intuitive and ordered by our roots, into the chaos caused by the passionate meeting with another person. This passage out of the relative safety and intrinsic logic of the animal kingdom is perhaps most poignantly portrayed in *Gone to Earth*, Mary Webb's second novel, written during the devastation of Europe by World War I.

"You was made bad," Hazel Woodus tells the tame fox she keeps, the motherless animal who is her primitive self, "and its queer-like to me, Foxy, as folk canna see that . . . (for) when you'm busy being a fox they say you'm a sinner!" Hazel, whose new peacock-blue dress of puberty must forever bear the indelible brown stain made by the blood of the hunted rabbit she tried to rescue while fleeing from her first sexual pursuer, suddenly is no longer able to see "herself throned above life and fate, as a child does. She saw that she was part of it all; she was mutable and mortal."

Though she scrubs long and hard at the mark which disfigures her dress it will not disappear. "As long as she wore the dress it would be there, like the stigma of pain that all creatures bear as long as they wear the garment of the flesh." Before the coming of adult sexual awareness, Hazel "had seen life go on, had heard of funerals, courtings, confinements and weddings in their conventional order—or reversed—and she had remained, as it were, intact. She had starved and slaved and woven superstitions, loved Foxy, and tolerated her father" and had never been driven into doubt or penetration of life's mysteries. She would never again know such safety.

Over and over, Mary Webb explores the suffering which

comes with higher consciousness, as inevitably, in her scheme of things, the replacement of trusting unity with the patterns and rhythms of nature by the complex activities caused by the coming of temporal love creates an overwhelming awareness of duality, human mortality, decay and death. The simplest things in the environment take on a vivid impact for the tormented lover, trying to find a meaning in the dark. Suddenly the shapes the shadows of the mountains make, the way the night birds talk, and the blowing masses of dead leaves in autumn become ominous reminders of the tenuous quality of existence, as the whole cosmos seems to shift and sway with threats of dissolution and disaster.

This is the period of the hardest struggle, symbolic in many ways of our whole struggle to be human, yet we cannot reach the higher joy of reunification with the universe unless we peer unflinchingly into the shadows of our doubt and keep the faith that somehow we will find the strength needed for survival and growth. In Mary Webb's writing the focus is always upon that period of lostness (even the town in *The Golden Arrow* is named Lostwithin) which gives birth to the spiritual stretching necessary to become reconciled to all life's contradictions, tragic twists, and deeper beauty. It is that period of troubled atheistic probing she so compassionately portrays which creates the underground poet in us all.

In novels where nature becomes personified and functions as a harbinger of human destiny, it is often the blowing wind that speaks of emptiness and opportunities misused. And it is invariably those people whose lives have turned to hollowness who cannot bear its howling, who must literally stop up their ears to keep away the memories and reprimands it seems to bring, the vision of the light that they once could have had and lost, which would have made all hardship and all emptiness seem bearable.

We hear the sorrow for those who never opened their

souls to love with all its pain, its darkness, and its ecstasy in
the roaring of the winds that encircle the blackened rock
formation on the mountain top, the dwelling of the absent
god, named "The Devil's Chair" by the local people. We
hear the mourning for all those who "had left things just as
they were" so that "with their will or without it the courses
of life flowed on to their undreamed of endings, from their
mysterious source." For according to the legend which forms
the thematic undercurrent of the book,

> every year . . . when the ghosses go to the Diafol,
> them as found the arrow come two by two, merry as
> whimbrels in a fine June. [However] there's a good
> few old women as come first, in the tale; like wold
> ancient brown trees they be, groping and muttering,
> some saying, "Accorns for the pigs, faggots for the
> fire; but we missed summat." And some saying,
> "We lived 'ard; we supped sorrow; we died re-
> spected; but we'm lonely." Then they all set up a cry
> like a yew-tree on a windy night: "Out o' mind! Out
> o' mind!" Then the ghosses stir like poplars, all grey
> and misty-like in a ring round the Chair, and there's
> no sound but sobbing.

Throughout Mary Webb's work, illuminating the sob-
bing, howling void, we find the presence of the light, the
perpetual "lan-thorne" of childhood, which, if only we can
keep it lit, will guide us through those thorny times of
danger and initiation. It is the Christian light of trust, of
homecoming and comfort, which her believers ignite in
order to appease the far more potent pagan forces of cruel
fate, of roaring wind and troubled waters. However, the line
of demarcation between the light which warms and illuminates and the fire that burns is very thin. For once the created
meaning which formed the source of the glow begins to

waver, the light rapidly turns into a fire that destroys all of
the material manifestations of our painfully extinguished
hopes. There are usually fires of epiphany interwoven with
the climaxes of the novels of Mary Webb, last expiations of
all that has turned empty. Yet these fires also seem to function as the final efforts of those who can no longer believe in
anything to violently blind themselves back into visionary
faith.

In *Precious Bane,* it is Beguildy the wizard, impotent in his
effect upon the course of human life, no longer able to evoke
miraculous happenings or to control the destiny of his own
family, who literally enacts the ancient threat of fire
of damnation, burning the materialistic future of Gideon, the
Sin Eater, from whom the inner light is also absent. Because
Gideon wanted to wed his daughter and wooed her away
successfully, Beguildy in his rage sets fire to the other
man's crops, creating a kind of cosmic doom for everyone
involved.

There was no barley now. Where it had been
were two great round housen made of white fire,
very fearful to see, being of the size and shape of the
stacks, but made of molten flame. There was no
substance in them, and it was a marvel how they
stood so. Now and again a piece of this molten stuff
would fall inward with no sound, and there could be
seen within caves of grey ash and red, sullen,
smouldering fire. So it will surely be when the
world is burned with fervent heat in the end of all.

In *The House in Dormer Forest,* it is the dying grandmother
who burns all of the contents of her own created past that
seem to be turning against her.

The clocks, the portraits, the nodding idol, the
stuffed animals, the Bibles and prayer-books in their

special bookcase—all these things seemed to crowd on her till she could not breathe. She felt at enmity with them. She wanted to get rid of them.

Inspired by the biblical text about "Burning and fuel of fire":

> She got up, took the candle, and went downstairs. The house was full of noises—the rats, the clocks, the rising night-wind, the little death-watches, ticking till the landing was like a clockmakers'. . . . With her huge nightcap, bare feet, and angry face she made a quaint picture. She lit a bonfire in the drawing-room, and another in the hall. Then she went back to bed very happily, feeling that she had removed all annoyance through the inspiration of a text. Upstairs, they all slept. Downstairs, the little fires crackled and blazed under the amazed eyes of the ancestors, and the glassy ones of the stuffed birds. The nodding idol disappeared in a welter of flame. The ancestors curled up in their frames.
>
> The rising moon laid the black shadow of the house on the lawn for the last time. Inside, it was already hollow. And now, within the shadow of the lawn, another shadow seemed to gather and stir and grow, so that what had been a quiet pool of darkness became like water when the wind goes over it. . . . The lower windows were all illuminated now, and Enoch, who was wakeful, having the sense of impending calamity shared by animals and poets, saw the angry, red glare.

And in *The Golden Arrow*, when Deborah is deserted by Stephen whom she has made into the meaning of her life, she drags all of the furniture which filled their little cottage underneath The Devil's Chair with warmth and light into the snow and burns it. However, after the blaze she uses to destroy all she once loved and hoped upon, in the ensuing darkness and the cold, it is again the little light of childhood, her "lan-thorne" which her father superstitiously keeps burning by her bedroom door which saves her. For in a trance-like state she gravitates towards it, makes the long journey home, and lives protected by her parents until Stephen can find his own light which allows him to return to her. Indeed, it is the sentimental singing of the Christian hymn, "Lead Kindly Light" which alone has the power to wake her to her tears of sorrow and mobility out of the death-like state of limbo she has placed herself in to avoid the knowledge of the pain of having been abandoned.

There is something very medieval about Mary Webb's tenuous juxtaposition of Christian belief upon a tangled lore of pagan folktales, the quality of interplay of darkness and illumination in her writing, that makes me think of the great Gothic cathedrals where the stained glass windows, those luminous flickerings of colored glass portraying all of human history, those multitudes of saints and sinners trying to make their little meanings, are set above a reverently hallowed high stone void. For built into the texture of her prose is the same reverence for those dark demonic forces, for the atheism and the doubt, that caused the medieval artisans to erect such massive cold-stone temples to the emptiness before adding the created color and the glow, man's daring effort to ascend into the light.

Down at the mine that morning Stephen had heard a thrush sing above a bed of early autumn violets in the manager's garden. . . . The idea of death, which every day of autumn had seemed to voice more insistently, which had haunted him since he had been flooded with the sense of nothingness, fled for a moment before the bird's voice. Stephen suddenly knew why he loved lights, colour, spring, song; why men built themselves warm houses and planted orchards; why women made their windows bright with geraniums and clean muslin; why mothers delighted in their babies and young men delighted in football and the zest of love. It was because all these things kept away the idea of death—the knowledge of a future intimacy with it; because they built up around the fleeting moment the sapphire walls of immortality.

Mary Webb, who from early childhood had watched the cruel mysterious ways of nature, spending every moment that she could outdoors, knew well the added pain of heightened perception. She was always drawn to the tragic in life and spent much of her time visiting poor cottages and workhouses. Even on the festive occasion of her wedding, held in the open air which was her drug, she chose for guests "the inmates of the women's ward of the workhouse she visited, an old herbalist who had endeared himself to her by his knowledge of plants, a poor old fellow who only possessed one sound eye, and a decrepit organ grinder."

She had grown up close to the desolate beauty of the wilds which drew her with such force that even in adulthood she could not leave her native Shropshire region long without being seized by what Hilda Addison, her first biographer, describes as a kind of cosmic homesickness reminiscent of Emily Bronte's insatiable longing for the Yorkshire Moors. As Addison points out, it was far more intense than the "normal longing to revisit old haunts," which is why, I think, her writings call to life the homesickness for childhood in us all with such a poignance.

Mary Webb best describes the addictive quality of her connection with the homeland in her characterization of Vessons, the caretaker of Undern Hall (in *Gone to Earth*), "a place of which the influence and magic were not good."

Ties deep as the tangled roots of the bindweed, strong as the great hawsers of the beeches that reached below the mud of Undern Pool, held him to it, the bondslave of a beauty he could not understand, a terror he could not express. When he trudged the muddy paths, "setting taters" or earthing up; when he scythed the lawn, looking, with a rose in his hat, weirder and more ridiculous than ever; and when he shook the apples down with a kind of sour humour, as if to say, 'There! that's what you trees get for having apples!'—at all these times he seemed less an individual than a blind force. For though his personality was strong, that of the place was stronger. Half out of the soil, minded like the doormouse and the beetle, he was, by virtue of his unspoken passion, the protoplasm of a poet.

Mary Webb, born Gladys Mary Meredith in 1881, was the first child of six. Her father was a Welsh schoolmaster and supposed descendant of Llwellyn, King of Wales, although that ancestry was never proved. Her mother, Sarah Alice Scott, had a distant kinship with the renowned Sir Walter. According to all accounts, Mary Webb led a cheerful and rather uneventful childhood at the Grange near Much Wenlock in the shadow of "the Wrekin," the hill that she always returned to. With her younger brothers and sister, or more often alone, she would take long hikes, would watch for Gypsies, or observe the excavation of a nearby ancient Roman wall. Despite repeated reprimands, she was unable to resist borrowing her mother's fancy clothing so that she could dress her siblings up as flowers or fairies in order to enact the plays she would make up. She was unusually tuned into other people's needs although somewhat oblivious to her own, especially in the matter of appearance, for though it pained her to be singled out, she was extremely careless

about her dress. Once a week she was sent into town to read
the Bible to Old John Lloyd, the beadle. And from the age of
ten, she had a governess, Miss Lory, who would read to her
from Shakespeare for hours on end.

The three years she spent at finishing school, from the age
of fifteen until she was eighteen, marked the first prolonged
absence from the beloved land where she grew up. When
she returned home, she was entrusted with the education of
her younger brothers and sisters, a task which she took very
seriously. Although there was no outward reason to worry,
she became increasingly nervous and worn out. Shortly after
her twentieth birthday she collapsed completely, a victim of
Graves' Disease and severe gastric troubles. She spent the
major portion of the next ten years in bed, asking that her
mattress be carried outside whenever the weather and her
health permitted.

Perhaps it was this period of sudden realization of her
own helpless frailty following such an unblighted childhood
which accelerated her understanding of the crucial issues of
decay and striving which were to form the underlay of all her
work. During those long years of enforced leisure, cut off
from the normal life, she read and wrote a great deal. It was
with great eagerness that she read A.E. Housman's *A Shropshire Lad,* Darwin's *The Origin of the Species,* and Haekel's *The
Riddle of the Universe,* trying to understand it all. She continued to write poetry and started to work upon her first collection of essays which was to be published later with an introduction by Walter de la Mare. Here we can feel the first
fusion of her inborn connectedness with nature with her
growing mystical philosophy.

Just as a certain air, introduced continually in a
piece of music, expresses the idea of the composer,
so this perceptual reincarnation of the same cabalistic signs in nature might help us, if we could gather

the scattered meanings, to a clearer understanding of
the plasmic force behind them—a force patient and
vast, vouchsafing no explanation. In this occult
script the world might find a new bible of spiritual
enlightenment—a writing not in fire upon tables of
stone, but in subtle traceries on young leaves and
buds. Have not all symbolic artists, children, and
priests of new religions some intuition of this? For
the thought—so dim and dear—that all fine con-
tours are a direct message from God, is rooted deep
in the minds of the simple-hearted, who are the
Magi of the world.

For Mary Webb, so long an invalid living close to the fear
of death, those impediments and infirmities which kept her
from the mainstream of human existence, which forced her to
reexamine the meaning of nature's patterns, became a catalyst of higher consciousness. Unable to join the unquestion-
ing masses and enjoy a normal youth, she gradually became
reconciled to her special role of seeing and expressing more
than most people. It is because of this, I feel, that she could
write so movingly of those whose poetic gifts isolate and
pain them, that through her fiction she could grant them
expiation from their suffering and grace. This isolation and
martyrdom of the seer became a theme of her fiction almost
immediately.

However it was a long time before she could deal directly
with the horror of actual deformity. Graves' Disease causes a
strange protrusion of the eyes which must have been particularly painful to a woman as hypersensitive to ridicule as
Mary Webb. In addition she suffered from a goiterous en-
largement of the throat, locally nicknamed "Derbyshire
neck." It was not until she had been married for many years
that she returned to face this early agony that had blighted
her own emerging womanhood, that she could let the up-

ward reaching soul of Prudence Sarn succeed, though her maimed appearance had set the whole world against her. For it is only after Mary Webb herself knows hope, that she can tell the story of her fears and aspirations, thinly veiled through Prue, in *Precious Bane.*

> And I ran away into the attic and cried a long while.
> But the quiet of the place, and the loneliness of it comforted me at long last . . . it being very still there, with the fair shadows of the apple trees peopling the orchard outside, that was void, as were the near meadows, Gideon being in the far field making hay-cocks, which I also should have been doing, there came to me, I cannot tell whence, a most powerful sweetness that had never come to me afore. It was not religious, like the goodness of a text heard at a preaching. It was beyond that. It was as if some creature made all of light had come on a sudden from a great way off; and nestled in my bosom. On all things there came a fair, lovely look, as if a different air stood over them. . . .
> I fell to thinking how all this blessedness of the attic came through me being curst. For if I hadna had a hare-lip to frighten me away into my own lonesome soul, this would never have come to me. The apples would have crowded all in vain to see a marvel, for I should never have known the glory that came from the other side of silence.

Later on in the novel, Mary Webb has Prue tell the reader

> it will seem strange . . . that a farm woman should look at things about her in this wise, and indeed it is not many do. But when you dwell in a house you mislike, you will look out of window a deal more

than those that are content with their dwelling. So I,
finding my own person and my own life not to my
mind, took my pleasure where I could.

What is it that makes *Precious Bane* so sacred and so
secret? I think it is Mary Webb's quite primal way of actual-
izing the bright side of human aspiration, making it "come
true," while painting in the darkest, wildest tones the terrors
of each tree, each crow and rook, personifying fears and
instincts most writers do not dare humanize. For, when we
consider the careful realism or the void abstraction of most
modern fiction, it is a rather grand and taboo thing to find
ourselves in the middle of a kind of medieval fairy story,
going towards a happy ending without sacrificing any modern knowledge of psychology.

There are no boundaries in *Precious Bane,* as, in the fairy
tale or certain deeply psychological fiction, all states of mind
are acted out. Rage burns up destinies. Fear shrivels people.
Prue's brother, Gideon, who eats bread over his father's
coffin in the tradition of the Sin Eaters of old, literally takes
on all of his father's worst qualities. All characters act out
their deepest drives and carry things to their ultimate conclusions as they act out the dramas of their intertwined, almost
incestuously intermingled lives. Yet simultaneously they *feel*
and react to everything they go through in the simplest,
deeply human, ways. All "His moments," (puppets), they
become humble observers of the catastrophic, almost cosmic
dramas they play parts in, awed watchers of their own inner
natures and of other life.

Set in a superstitious rural area of former times near the
border of Wales, where curses passed down over generations of family battles, and where plagues and winds and
troubled waters lie heavy on the hearts of humans trying to
know the meaning of their destinies, *Precious Bane* takes the
quest for survival of the good into its most mythical propor-

tions. As the unutterably beautiful and evil-ridden world around unfolds, Prue Sarn, who as an isolated growing child has been at one with nature, not knowing her differentness and loving everything, must slowly come to know the sorrow of her curse.

As she goes to the village inn, ecstatic at her first adult outing into the world beyond, in her heart she hears the people she was looking at with pleasure cry:

> "Her be a wench turns into a hare by night."
> "Her's a witch, an ugly, hare-shotten witch."
> "Dunna drink while she's by. It'll p'ison yer innards. . . . You'll dwine and dwine away."
> The folk inside looked at each other, and I wished I could die. . . . For indeed I loved my kind and would lief they had loved me. . . . For they were part of my outing and part of Lullingford and of the world, that ever seized my heart in its hands, as a child will hold a small bird, which is both affrighted and comforted to be so held. I would lief have ridden forth and seen new folk, new roads, new hamlets, children playing on strange village greens, unknown to me as if they were fairies, come there I knew not whence nor how, singing their songs and running away into the dusk.

Though the enlarging world would imprison Prue Sarn, would make her slave to her deformity, her spirit continues to grow. Though local superstitions around her person also keep growing and harm comes to the people she loves the best, she still continues to feel good and giving. Even when the crops she's worked so hard to cultivate go up in flames caused by the wild and complicated wrath of all of those who sought only to reap, she can remember how it was the sowing she loved best, the

swinging out our arms with a great giving movement, as if we were feeding all the world, a thing I
dearly loved to see. For reaping, though it is good to
watch as be all the year's doings on a farm, is a
grutching and a grabbing thing compared with sowing. You must lean out to it and sweep it in to you,
and hold it to your bosom, jealous, and grasp it and
take it. There is ever a greediness in reaping with the
sickle, in my sight. There is not in scything, which is a
large destroying movement without either love or
anger in it, like the judgments of God. Nor is there in
flailing, which is a thing full of anger, but without any
will or wish to have or keep. But reaping is all greed,
just as sowing is all giving. For there you go, up and
down the wide fields, bearing that which you have
saved. . . . And though it is all you have, you care not,
but take it in great handfulls and cast it abroad, with
no thought of holding back any.

How Prue Sarn manages to forge on without withering
and withholding, without becoming saccharine or sacrificing
her ever-increasing insight, though she is involved in the
most hideous and disillusioning dramas, is the true miracle
of this book and perhaps what most attracts us about it. For
Prue never becomes passive. Rather, in the style of the true
hero of a fairy tale she does everything from killing a dog at
a bull baiting to prevent a cruelty, to posing naked on a
rising platform concealed by a smoke puff to impersonate a
resurrected Venus to save a wizard's daughter from shame.
And through the fullest participation her deformity threatened to deny, she learns the compassion for her fellow humans that allows her to live with their flaws, appreciate their
better qualities, and somehow triumph on her own.

We feel in reading *Precious Bane,* Prue Sarn must triumph,
the ecstatic way that she experiences beauty must help her

break through her earthly shell. Each year at the time of the troubling of the waters, she goes to Sarn Mere to watch the dragonflies "come out of their bodies," translucent and transformed.

> We had a power of dragon-flies at Sarn, of many kinds and colours, little and big. But every one was bound in due season to climb up out of its watery grave and come out of its body with great labour and pain, and a torment like the torment of childbirth, and a rending like the rending of the tomb. . . . And the lilies there, "When they were buds, they were like white and gold birds sleeping, head under wing, or like summat carven out of glistening stone, or, as I said afore, they were like gouts of pale wax. But when they were come into full blow they wunna like anything but themselves, and they were so lovely you couldna choose but cry to see them."

And so too we could cry for Prue, who in her unique beauty of soul isn't like anything but herself, who in the strength and wisdom she acquires through her tragedy, her "bane," transcends all those more fortunately fated. And so, also, we feel that Mary Webb is telling us, we shall all come out of the prisons of our bodies and the limitations of the life around us, if only we can love enough to act.

Tragedy comes windingly to those who fail to find their sense of higher purpose, to Prue's brother Gideon, the "Sin Eater" who drives everyone that he encounters nigh to death in the blind furthering of his own materialistic aims, to the innocently beautiful Jancis whose lips make a rose whenever she says "O," and even to Prue's mother who has never learned to forgive herself for the fact that "a hare crossed her path" when she was pregnant.

One by one, the others are overcome by the forces of their hopelessly tangled destinies, until Prue alone, accused of

being the witch who caused it all, is rescued from the ritual
drowning on the ducking-stool the townspeople decree to be
her fate, by the wandering weaver, saint, and seer, who can
penetrate beneath the surface of things as they seem.

How pure and simple is the ending of the tale.

"But no!" I said. . . . "You mun marry a girl like a
lily. See, I be hare-shotten!"

But he wouldna listen. He wouldna argufy. Only
after I'd pleaded agen myself a long while, he pulled
up sharp, and looking down into my eyes, he said—

"No more sad talk! I've chosen my bit of Paradise. 'Tis on your breast, my dear acquaintance!"

And when he'd said those words, he bent his
comely head and kissed me full upon the mouth.

. . . .

Here ends the story of Prudence Sarn.

Is *Precious Bane* possible? Written as if it is, it gives the
dreamer in us all the chance to forge on, hoping that despite
the obstacles we can build ourselves a future in which our
inner goodness will be kissed and seen, will lead us to those
places that we want the most to go. We want life to have a
fairy tale ending. Over and over we struggle with the last
lines of the *Diary of Anne Frank*, thinking surely her insistence
that "I still believe people are basically good at heart" ought
to be able to be heard and heeded so she can survive and
thrive. We want the ending to reverse.

But what Mary Webb gives us is more than the archetypal
happy ending of the fairy tale, where transformations come
to princesses and princes trapped in bear and frog skins,
where the kiss from one who sees the trapped creature as
beautiful sets the real beauty free. For when the princely

weaver kisses Prudence Sarn upon the spot of her deformity, it does not go away, she does not shed it suddenly. Rather, the blemish, loved and kissed at last, can make her whole and open up the gates of entry to the joys it threatened to deny. Thus what is finally evoked in us is more than the fairy tale longing that our inner beauty will be seen so clearly it will make us beautiful before the world, it is the longing to be known and loved for all our blemishes, our warts and wens and contradictions, to be "let in" whole. Thus *Precious Bane* becomes the secret gift, our deepest dream.

When Mary Webb first started to write fiction, her tales poured out with such rapidity that her husband had to buy her a special fountain pen with an accelerated ink flow. She wrote the whole of *The Golden Arrow* in three weeks and found that her most hurriedly composed passages were invariably her strongest. When she was writing, she would become possessed and oblivious to all things practical. Her mother claimed that when she stayed with her she could never be sure of a meal unless she herself fixed it, nor was her gaining entrance to the cottage guaranteed. Although her mother provided her with a substantial allowance, Mary Webb and her husband generally lived from hand to mouth. According to her two biographers, Hilda Addison and Thomas Moult, this poverty was due in great measure to her incorrigible charity rather than the kind of desperate need that fires the imaginations of those who wish to romanticize the artist's life. Apparently a "gentle stream of 'down and outs' discovered Spring Cottage" and its owner's good will. Upon one occasion a laborer's daughter asked Mary Webb for a piano and got it. Another time she made arrangements for a consumptive boy and his entire family to be resituated at the seaside.

To compensate for the precarious financial position this

overflowing generosity brought about, Mary Webb would
garden hard in wind and rain, alternating this labor with her
writing. Once a week she would take the fruit and flowers
that she grew nine miles into the nearest town to market.
Rising many hours before dawn, she would first offer the
apples on her wheelbarrow to her neighbors, who, by and
large, seemed to accept her rather eccentric lower-class way
of life. Then she would continue to her stall where she
would stand just like Prue Sarn, peddling her roses and her
gillyflowers while she listened to the local tales that fill her
fiction.

By the time *Precious Bane* came out in 1924, Mary Webb
had already received a fair measure of recognition. Rebecca
West had called attention to her work in 1917 and Thomas
Hardy, whose tragic vision she felt very close to, had read
her writing with respect. She had written to Hardy for permission to dedicate her final novel to him, and had received
an affirmative answer. Now, ironically, the *Dictionary of Literary Biography* ends its short synopsis of Mary Webb's accom-
plishments with the cryptic remark that she "could not be
Hardy" because "a naive primitive quality" about her work
"prevented it from ever attaining tragic stature."

Although Mary Webb wrote *Seven for a Secret* after *Precious
Bane,* as Thomas Moult points out, she knew that *Precious
Bane* was her lifework, that all else was merely a prelude.
Unfortunately, this work that meant so much to her was not
treated too kindly by the book reviewers of her day. The
principal literary journal from which the others took their
cues complained that "it requires a deal of imagination to
believe that Prue Sarn, however straight the furrows she
ploughed, would be likely to write" with the poetic vision
Mary Webb endowed her with. Elsewhere the book was
described as a "pleasantly ambitious work of fiction. But it is
not sufficiently in the spirit of our time to awaken more than

a 'literary' interest in the reader." Although Edward Pugh declared it a masterpiece, he "cried in the wilderness."

Thanks to Pugh's efforts, the following year *Precious Bane* was awarded the "Femina La Vie Heureuse" Prize for the best imaginative work of fiction by an author who had not gained sufficient recognition. However she never quite recovered her spiritual strength. Her mother died that year, a loss which had an adverse effect upon her already rapidly deteriorating health. She became very dependent upon her moods and began to let whole weeks go by without working upon her major projects, although she continued to contribute short stories and reviews to London periodicals.

Unlike her early works, which once begun proceeded with astonishing speed, *Armour Wherein He Trusted,* her final piece of fiction written in archaic dialect, went very slowly. After nearly two years of effort, it was only half completed. Then one day, her friend Mr. Adcock, the editor of *Bookman,* received a call from her to say she was unwell and in a fit of hopelessness had thrown the uncompleted manuscript into the fire. Over the telephone he heard the "sound of subdued stifled crying." In a tragic way, as often happens in the life of writers, she had predicted her own fate; as like the characters she wrote about, she tried to destroy her created meaning by burning, after it turned vacuous. Although the manuscript was rescued, when she left London for Shrewsbury she hardly added anything to it, so it remains a fragment.

The last thing that Mary Webb wrote, a review of a novel by Edith Wharton, contained these lines: "After all, who is afraid of a dead leaf in winter? Only in the rose gardens of summer is it a threat!" She was in her mid-forties at the time and dying. Aware of her precarious hold on life, her friends advised her to stop working and break with all her old surroundings and the disappointments of the literary world. She decided to stay with Miss Lory, the beloved governess

who had read Shakespeare to her when she was growing up.
But by the time she arrived at her destination of St. Leo-
nards-on-Sea, she had collapsed from the strain of the long
trip. She had to be carried off the train by the railway offi-
cials and was taken straight to a nursing home.

For a moment she looked out of the window at the waters
where the sun was setting and proclaimed that the beauty
would make her better. But then she turned away, buried her
head, and cried. During those last few days she became
particularly sentimental about the flowers people brought to
her, reminders of the land she loved. Her husband brought
her a lily from her own plant and other people brought her
violets which she would kiss and cuddle to her throat as if
their radiance of life could save her. On October 8, 1927,
she died of pernicious anemia and a recurrence of Graves'
Disease.

In the Berg Collection of the New York Public Library,
there is a thin, handwritten manuscript wrapped up in leather
binders entitled "Poetry of the Prayer Book." In it Mary
Webb describes praying as "launching a wireless message in
space. . . . Where it will go [we] cannot guess. Who will pick
it up, how many will hear it, who will reply to it, how long it
will go echoing away and away into the dark—all this is
unknown. . . . but does [the] message fail to be heard on that
account? Surely not! Whoever is waiting for it will get it!"
And so I feel about Mary Webb's writing itself, which came
to me as such a message that perhaps I can pass on, those
dear dust-covered volumes lost in long obscurity.

AN ELEGY FOR
DJUNA BARNES

On Friday, June 18, 1982, Djuna Barnes died in Patchin Place where she had lived as a recluse for many years. I never saw her when she was alive. By chance my thirteen-year-old daughter was at a party right above her Greenwich Village apartment when they brought her body out. She had never seen a dead person before and was frightened. She told me how they wheeled her out, all wrapped in plastic. She told me it was Djuna Barnes. And suddenly, before I knew what I was saying, I had said, "How beautiful!"

There is a very minor character in Djuna Barnes's *Nightwood* who is tattooed from head to toe with angels and obscenities, historical quotations, vulgarities, and magic incantations. When asked "why all this barbarity; he answered he loved beauty and would have it about him."

The writings of Djuna Barnes, filled with the dissonances of a deteriorating age, the undertows of ugliness that haunt us all, call for a serious redefinition of the concept of beauty, and of the value of intensity, of authentic experience of the dark side of existence from which we flee. The Sunday after my daughter saw Djuna Barnes in her final earthly passing, the obituary pages of the New York Times summed up *Nightwood*, the main opus she left to the world, calling it a "story about a psychopathic woman who destroys those nearest her—her husband, her son, two women who love her [which] is told, Greek chorus style by a physician." That is all.

Thus "a recluse whose avant-garde literary work won wide acclaim in the 1920's and 30's" is put to rest, as is her tumultuous disturbing genius, while our audiences continue to read nonfiction explorations of autism, and anorexia, biographies of terrorists, concentration-camp victims, corrupt politicians, and utopian dreamers, bemoaning the fact that by and large the urge to write powerful fiction has left the modern milieu. And perhaps it has.

In this age of psychic numbing, when we are just beginning to wake ourselves to the images and meanings of the Holocaust of forty years ago, and are still hiding from facing the possibility of a Holocaust to come and the full responsibility of trying to free ourselves from it, we seem to only be able to take in a certain combination of pain and passion in a nonfiction form which eliminates the distance between the self and what is being told. And yet, as we know from the Greek drama, it is only in daring to bridge that safe distance between the creator/creation and the audience, that art can break through the barriers of what we fear to know yet must. Precisely because Djuna Barnes is so disturbing, and because we live in an age in which we must be disturbed in order to survive, now, a few months after her death, before she is too safely put to rest, I would like to say again some of what I said in *Book Forum* in 1977, when it was our concern to try to rescue this then still-living writer from an already descending obscurity.

At the time a new bibliography for "Barnes scholars" had just been published by David Lewis, edited by Douglas Messerli, in which Messerli pointed out that although Djuna Barnes had an acknowledged influence on Dylan Thomas, Faulkner, Eliot, Durrell, Lowry, Crane, and perhaps Joyce, whom she introduced to the American expatriates in Paris, today, even in the universities, few were familiar with her writing. Messerli ventured, "There are several reasons why Djuna Barnes has yet to be universally appreciated, the most obvious of which is the complexity and elusiveness of her work. From the very beginning, the difficulty of her stories and plays attracted some critics while repelling others."

And yet, when I read the collection of excerpts from works about Barnes, reviews and critical essays, which constituted the second half of the bibliography, it became increasingly clear that it was not the intellectual, philosophical, or stylistic "difficulty" which deterred a more widespread appreciation of this acknowledged genius of the English language. The "difficulty" was of a far more subtle yet more devious nature and had to do with our acceptance of the validity of pain as an experience within a culture which places a high premium upon comfort and contentment. It had to do with the poetic revelation of obsessions which violate all limits and taboos.

For considering the stark literature to which we have grown accustomed, the bleak everyday world of the realists, the desolate vision of the existentialists, and the unredeemed vulgarity of the pornographers, it seemed rather incongruous to find reviewer after reviewer (and the *Times* obituary writer proved no exception), unable to question Djuna Barnes's brillance of style, railing at her "uncompromising bitterness," her "comfortless vision," the "decadence" and "perversion" of her world views, not noticing the passion underlying her prose, not noticing that *Nightwood* is one of the most moving love stories in Western literature.

Often Djuna Barnes has been compared to Beckett because of her seeming bitterness. However, her works are in striking contrast to his, in which the arbitrary configurations of our world which cause emotional numbness and brutality are shown in all of their contradictory nature, making all human hope seem futile. Unlike Beckett, for whom emotional distance is the only defense against an unalterably irrational outer world, for whom alienation reflected in stark language and barren landscaping is the only protection against psychic annihilation, Djuna Barnes enters the irrational with her eyes wide open, gathering elaborate imagery of every era as she goes, fully surrendering to its forces, following its call. By participating as a poet in a pattern too terrifyingly vast for comprehension, she creates the passions that transcend the fear of pain which prevents our full experience of our existence. By giving herself over to that pattern with a reverence which is almost religious, making even its profanity sacred through her art, she transforms what could be helplessness to awe.

Djuna Barnes began as a journalist around 1913, writing and drawing for such publications as the Brooklyn *Daily Eagle,* the New York *Press,* the *Morning Telegraph,* and *Charm* magazine. Among the nearly 200 articles which date from this period we find such titles as "The Tingling, Tangling Tango as 'Tis Tripped at Coney Isle," "Sad Scenes on Sentence Day in the Kings County Court; The Strangest Part of This Drama of Life is the Audience, Made Up of Shiftless Men Who Never Seem to Tire of Listening to the Tales of the Fallen and Vicious," "How It Feels to Be Forcibly Fed," and "Woman Police Deputy Writer of Poetry; Mrs. Ellen O'Grady Not so Keen about Freud, but Believes in the Psychological Moment; Ardently Interested in Her Special Task of Preventing Sex Crime and Confident of Eventual Success." The range of subjects of these early articles, testifying to a thorough apprenticeship in the ways of human nature

becoming increasingly rare among today's fiction writers,
calls to mind the years that Dostoyevsky spent in night
court, the hours Mann spent witnessing the public demon-
strations of the early psychoanalysts, and Balzac's sojourns
in French society in between feverish bouts of writing in
isolation.

By the end of World War I, Djuna Barnes's short stories,
poetry, and plays were appearing in American magazines
and newspapers, both popular and literary, and later, during
the twenties, in the leading expatriate journals. In the late
twenties she became active in the Theater Guild and wrote
extensively for *Guild* magazine.

By 1936 when *Nightwood* came out in England, originally
entitled *Bow Down*, Djuna Barnes had already published
three books: *A Book* (1923: reissued as *A Night Among the
Horses* in 1929), *Ladies Almanack* (published anonymously in
Paris in 1928, recently reissued by Harper & Row), and a
best selling novel, *Ryder* (1928). In 1937 *Nightwood* was
published in this country with an introduction by T.S. Eliot.
The publication of *Nightwood* abruptly marked the end both
of Djuna Barnes's career in journalism and her public life. It
was not until 1958 that Djuna Barnes published *The Anti-
phon*, a complex poetic drama which was translated into
Swedish by Dag Hammarskjold and produced at the Swedish Royal Dramatic Theater. During the last two decades of
her life, although she continued to write, she published very
little.

Because of the barriers against the emotional areas explored in Djuna Barnes's work, the reluctance to bare those
inner recesses of being from which our pain and passion
come, there has been a widespread tendency to dismiss her
writing as incomprehensible rather than face its deeper
meaning. Even those critics who have recognized the literary
importance of *Nightwood* have concentrated more upon its
structure and its language than its content.

In *Nightwood* inner realities are acted out, complicated interpersonal and situational relationships are carried to their ultimate conclusions, and agony is not ignored. It is the fear of pain which we must pass through in order to achieve true spiritual sensation which causes so many readers to flee from this book. It is the fear of the forbidden desire for divinity contained in all of us, the desire for merging with the forbidden sex and the forbidden past.

Caged in a carefully tapestried intellectual and imagistic framework, *Nightwood* is the story of a homosexual love which is all-consuming. Not since Proust, who changed the genders of his characters to make his story acceptable to his readers, has the spiritual nature of the homosexual experience been rendered with such intensity. In *Nightwood* it is through homosexual merging that the stripping of the layers which insulate the characters from their own unconscious lives occurs. Speaking of her overwhelming love for Robin, Nora says, "A man is another person—a woman is yourself, caught as you turn in panic; on her mouth you kiss your own. If she is taken you cry that you have been robbed of yourself. God laughs at me, but his laughter is my love."

There is a heightening of awareness which comes only at enormous risk. Nora Flood is the lover without defenses, who "robbed herself for everyone; incapable of giving herself warning, she was continually turning about to find herself diminished. . . . Cynicism, laughter, the second husk into which the shucked man crawls, she seemed to know little or nothing about."

Robin who is loved not only by Nora but by Felix, the wandering Jew in search of roots he cannot find, surrounded by rich red velvet brocades and borrowed vestiges of royalty, becomes the missing inner core of everyone, more present in her imprint than her flesh. She is "La Somnambule" whose waking sleep is "a decay fishing her beneath the visible surface." Even the unseen songbirds which surround her bed are covered to still their song at night. "Stepping in the trepidation of flesh that will become myth; as the unicorn is neither man nor beast deprived, but human hunger pressing its breast to its prey," Robin is a "woman who is beast turning human" who must follow the rhythms of an inner night which no one yet can know.

As the statue in Nora's garden becomes more itself with the erosions of the wind and rain, and less the sculptor's, as each finds his own location only in another's memories, and only through the anticipation of great loss can fullest love be known, each of the characters in *Nightwood* undergoes the slow "decay" towards other older sides of self and imprints of generations long gone which leads to future destiny. Within each new union are embodied the forces of eventual separation. Within each ecstatic merging the prospect of the coming loneliness is contained.

Sometimes Nora and Robin "would fall into an agonized embrace, looking into each other's face, their two heads in their four hands, so strained together that the space that divided them seemed to be thrusting them apart. Sometimes in these moments of insurmountable grief Robin would make some movement, use a peculiar turn of phrase not habitual to her, innocent of the betrayal by which Nora was informed that Robin had come from a world to which she would return. To keep her (in Robin there was this tragic longing to be kept, knowing herself astray) Nora knew that there was no way but death."

Robin is stolen from Nora by Jenny Petherbridge, "The Squatter," a collector of other people's wedding rings, mementos, and important meanings. Because Jenny is empty inside and can only have "second hand dealings with life," she appropriates Nora's passion as the most vibrant emotional involvement she has seen. Searching for Robin's new mistress, Nora finds the right location by coming upon a doll propped up against the bed pillows, remembering that Robin once gave her a doll. "We give death to a child when we give it a doll—it's the effigy and the shroud; when a woman gives it to a woman, it is the life they cannot have, it is their child; sacred and profane."

Richer yet bereaved, Nora returns to the doctor who once delivered her to ask about the vastness of the night into which Robin disappeared. Dr. Matthew-Mighty-grain-of-salt-Dante-O'Connor is the seer who is forced to witness all, but like "The Squatter" cannot feel. He is the "uninhabited angel" who lies in bed dressed as the woman that he cannot be, the false magician who must rouge his lips and cheeks so that his face may seem to come alive. He is almost an anti-God in his premature perception of the patterns which he cannot alter, as he himself repeatedly becomes the catalyst for the events, the meetings, and betrayals which lead into ever more inextricable entanglements. Despite his long and often cruel poetic monologues on human suffering and striving, he is strangely untouchable.

His relationship with Nora is highly charged because on some deep level he craves her very vulnerability, her ability to give herself over to passion, and perhaps even her pain. He tells her that she is "experiencing the inbreeding of pain. Most of us do not dare it. We wed a stranger, and so 'solve' our problem. But when you inbreed with suffering (which is merely to say that you have caught every disease and so pardoned your flesh) you are destroyed back to your structure as an old master disappears beneath the knife of the scientist who would know how it was painted."

In this passage, Djuna Barnes is also describing the danger and the greatness of her own writing which forces the reader into areas of confrontation with the self from which all comforting defenses are absent. Through portraying so ardently the passion evoked by Nora's loss, she is creating a higher spiritual state in which even tragedy is merely a matter of definition and living fully may be the ultimate reality. She is inviting us to dare to take the risk of going on her voyage.

The resistance of contemporary readers to the intensity of the voyage of Djuna Barnes and to the insistence with which she faces the night side of our inner lives is understandable in light of the climate of our culture. The inhumane atrocities of our century have caused such a wide scale of psychic numbing that collectively we have become like the autistic individual who must shut out all feeling and response in order to be spared the inevitably recurring disappointments. Fearful of real touching, we have created mass sensitivity groups in which contact loses its individual sacredness. Fearful of responsibility for our unconscious journeys, we have turned to drugs that bring sensation divorced from our conscious wills.

Because deepest despair embodies in it elements of hope and resurrection, as pain embodies in its essence joy and passion, in defense against a literature of false hope there has been a tendency in modern fiction to depersonalize despair. Generally, truly disturbing imagery occurs in contemporary writing only when it is disengaged from beauty and expression. However, it is only through the element of beauty that pain portrayed in art acquires the familiarity that allows it to penetrate our inner core, become part of us, and change us. And much as we rail against being violated by intensity, on a deeper level we cannot be satisfied with the safety and abstraction of impersonality.

In order to survive this century, we must be willing to look upon many truths about the dark side of our human nautre with our eyes wide open. We must be willing to probe those truths to their darkest source, to feel them and to ponder them. Djuna Barnes, who could hold on to our human poetry and hope even with her eyes wide open to the horrors of the modern world and of the human soul itself, is a writer who must be read and kept alive, now more than ever in her death.

A PLEA FOR
IMPASSIONED
REVIEWING

ecently a psychoanalyst whom I very much admire, describing an experimental play that she had seen, told me about her resistance to the use of the theatrical amphitheater for what she termed "manipulation of the audience." Although she is an active fighter in her field against the psychic numbing and indifference so prevalent in our society, she was angered by a work of art that attempted to engulf the viewer and destroy the element of critical distance.

It has been so very long since art has been accepted as a source of magical transformation, involving a total and trusting surrender of self on the part of the spectator and a total giving of self on the part of the creator, that we are shockingly inexperienced in being profoundly moved. We fear the possibility of being altered, of allowing our reactions to get

out of control. When literature affects us deeply, we immedi-
atley want to be able to define its power rationally, to lessen
its impact, as it were, by dividing its whole into a series of
comprehensible parts which will allow us to place it within a
familiar and nonthreatening framework. Although we wish
to be enriched by the books we read, we do not want to take
the risk of full immersion in the subjective vision of "the
other" or be possessed by oceanic currents of emotion that
will set off our own carefully submerged obsessions.

In this the modern critic serves us well. His is the science of demystification in all of its dimensions. He has
relinquished his role of pathfinder for that of censor and
judge. By providing us with the objectivity to analyze and
evaluate the strengths and weaknesses of a given work, the
critic is protecting us from forfeiting our own autonomy
and distance.

Although we recognize that some of the finest literary
criticism of the past was done by writers with a deep personal affinity for the works which they wrote about, often
even by close personal friends of the writers, we ask our
critics to be absolutely impartial and uninvolved, so that the
value judgments which they ultimately arrive at will be as
pure as possible.

Perhaps if we could become less interested in placing
value judgments and more concerned about the meaning of
literature as a form of sharing of perceptions on all levels,
our reviewers would be free again to write about the works
they love the most, for indeed it is the reviewer who is most
affected by a particular piece of writing who can best illumi-
nate the journey towards the understanding of it, if true
understanding is what we seek, rather than the arbitrary
assigning of importance or lack of it.

If we could rid ourselves of the competitive hierarchical
system which now dominates the literary world, where each
new work must be assigned a specific place upon the ladder

of success, we would be able to turn our energies towards
discovering the spiritual and human realms contained in
writings and their relevance to us as readers. Then the reviewer would no longer have to function as a barrier between the reader and the writer by writing about works
which do not touch a personal chord. If reviewers were to
write only about works to which they felt meaningfully connected, they would be able to offer deeply experienced accounts of their discoveries to potential readers with similar
affinities and the books that sometimes fall by the wayside
would be more likely to find the proper audience.

A more compassionate mode of criticism based upon affinities would also eliminate the tendency of most reviewers
to concentrate upon the unsuccessful aspects of the works
which are considered. The current system of evaluation and
elaborate technical dissection creates a relatively safe field of
operation for writings of recognizable merit which do not
deviate greatly from the norms and standards which we have
set up. However, it creates numerous dangers for truly innovative works, which often in their reaching out towards
new forms are flawed, especially in the early stages of any
given writer's development.

In striving towards the unattainable, which is a quality we
recognize in all great works of art in retrospect, the writer
must explore previously uncharted realms. The more cosmic
the aspirations, the more possible pitfalls will be encountered in the shaping of the final product. Knowing already what they have become, we are more than willing to
forgive James Joyce and Virginia Woolf for the slight awk-
ward moments in their early works. But we refuse to show
the same generosity of spirit to the writers of the current
generation. While bitterly complaining that there are no important works of fiction presently being written, we attack
our more far-reaching writers by focusing upon their imper-
fections, refusing to recognize the often blurred paths of their

trajectories, refusing to have faith that they will someday get where they are trying to go. Ironically, it is to the efforts of those writers who are able to consistently maintain their inborn water levels that we give the most support, those writers who, in the words of Emerson, never dared to "hitch their wagons to a higher star."

In writing only about the works that they find most compelling, impassioned reviewers have it in their power to re-establish the lost function of literature as a mode of deep spiritual communication. Potentially reviewers might use their critical gifts to help contemporary readers suspend their disbelief, so that in the manner of ancient audiences they will be able to enter the many underworlds of writing in a ritual of true communion.

Perhaps too, given an atmosphere of increased public trust and nurturance, more modern writers will become willing to make the harrowing and lonesome voyage into the depths of the unconscious from which great literature can grow.

A PLEA FOR
INTELLECTUAL
RISK-TAKING

ecently a social scientist I know became ready to publish her first full-length study. She had already been much courted by experts in her discipline, as well as by the popular media. For during her years of fieldwork she had made many fascinating discoveries. She possessed a great deal of coveted factual information.

Sight unseen, her manuscript had experts and major academic presses vying with one another to bring it to light. Enormous interest existed among those in powerful, prestigious positions. The trouble was, in the course of accruing the information that was clearly such a desirable commodity, the young social scientist had also found reason to question the very intellectual concepts which form the bedrock of her discipline. What she had seen, recorded, and experienced formed a whole new theoretical base which it would take a lifetime to explore. She knew that she was barely beginning and her ground was still shaky. The largeness of her own new formulations both excited her and frightened her. Although she knew her approach was unorthodox, she felt that if indeed her work was valid it could have widespread ramifications.

She was nervous about how the experts who had offered her such glowing opportunities would greet the theories in the total manuscript which grew out of the research that so fascinated them. Her fears were not unfounded. The experts who had vied with one another for her manuscript, having gone over it, agreed to support it only if she separated the concrete information that they wanted from the far more controversial theories that first motivated her to seek it. It was suggested that if perhaps she wanted to include an appendix of tentative tame conclusions, and an introduction making clear that they could be ignored, she would be serving her own academic interests.

Everyone agreed that to present a controversial theory at this early stage in her career would only get a lot of people angry. People who cared about her future suggested that she first publish her field study without any novel interpretations, a course of action that would assure her a positive reception, prestige, public lecture tours, and glowing book reviews. Then later, if she still believed in her own theories, she would have the "clout" to publish them in still another book without risking such dire consequences. Although her ideas might still antagonize, she would be in a much better position to fight back.

When I last spoke to the young social scientist, she was already making the revisions that would bring the support she had been promised to further her career. The criticisms of the experts, with their years of theory formulating and experience behind them, had of course cut very deep. And the more she complied with them, winning praise, the more she wondered if the basic premise which both grew out of and helped to motivate her research was worth any further thought.

What does this mean for all of us as human beings on the planet striving to unearth and understand and know? If indeed the young social scientist's theories are fallacious, we have been spared the mental hardship of confronting them and being forced to figure out where she went wrong. We have also been spared the mental exercise of confronting a body of ideas that might turn all we hold familiar topsy-turvy and force us to think things through again in order to establish our own positions.

We are so frightened by ideas that seem to lead us off in the wrong direction. It is as if we have learned to perceive the human mind as so vulnerable and so weak that any misconception or misinformation could destroy its functioning forever. Yet it is only through being mentally derailed and jarred that our complacency is broken and new concepts given space for breaking through.

The approach to scholarship that asked the social scientist to extricate the questions and personal preoccupations underlying her research from her final presentation is ultimately a selfish one. For we as readers and as curious fellow humans, when we are offered only carefully pre-sifted facts, are deprived of sharing in the whole process through which questions, raw materials, and possibilities of answers cause an explorer of new realities to forge forward. We are deprived of understanding the faltering, yet vivid-breathing method through which intellectual breakthroughs can be made.

For given only ironclad, already-proven theories, too well armored to penetrate or attribute to flawed, uncertain humans like ourselves, we become more and more wary of the amorphous nature of our own ground-breaking thought. Given only "answers," we stop asking the kinds of questions which will lead us onto shaky ground.

We have only to watch a small child mocking a still smaller child for "asking stupid questions" (inevitably those questions are the ones that deal with the meaning of our existence on the most primal and philosophic level) to see how early and completely those wonderings which no amount of factual mastery can put to rest are hammered out of us. And yet only out of the simplest questions can we touch upon profound wisdom.

The social scientist describing her work had said, "My central theory is so simple, it is ridiculous. Yet, if it is true, it could be so exciting." This, I think, is true for all important thought.

Yet we are uneasy around ideas that seem too simple-minded. Our brains, long trained in the burden of retaining complicated information and categorizing into manageable size complex bodies of thought, often do not seem tough enough to hold ideas that do not fit into definite parameters of preplanned molds as to what thinking ought to be.

We are so terrified of being confused, or led in the wrong direction, that each new body of ideas, once it is finally let through, becomes a dogma, a giant barricade to ward off any concept threatening to rattle it.

All breakthrough is frightening. In shattering the explanations which allow us some small comfort against the tremendous void of the unknown, we often are plunged into a transitory darkness, until new ideas and explanations start to jell. And yet we crave also to grow in understanding, and to learn, explain, and know.

I decided to go to visit Dorothy Dinnerstein, to talk to her about breakthrough into the realms of ideas that frighten us.

Her first book, *The Mermaid and the Minotaur: Sexual Arrangements and Human Malaise,* had predicted the doom of our entire species and our planet if we remain unwilling to alter radically the gender patterns that have crippled us. Because Dorothy Dinnerstein's root theory is based upon the most primal mother/infant ties, universal in all human societies, and upon the fact that the very tie (not the way in which it is expressed, which presumably could be more easily worked with) is the cause of the destructive way that men and women relate to each other, reading her book forces us to fully acknowledge the gravity of our current dilemma. Had she chosen to fixate upon the nature of oppression of women by men, of all people by governments, or the shortcomings of certain methods of mothering, her study would have been far less "depressing." We would have had the satisfaction of accepting or rejecting possible solutions we could easily incorporate into our own patterns of thinking. However, given all of human history where mothering by women is accepted as natural, profound, and extremely beautiful, how do we cope when we are clearly shown that, no matter what the political and social changes in our world, male babies will make the necessary separation from the first nurturer that they need in order to survive by turning all their ambivalence outward toward the other sex, while forever wishing to be dependent upon it, never learning how to fully and dearly love it, while female babies will make the "Other," the male, the "all good" love object and turn all of the ambivalence and rage against the self? If indeed, as Dorothy Dinnerstein believes, this is the cause of the uneasy "collaboration" which makes all humans live in dependency, hatred, and fear, nothing short of a total transformation of our child-rearing patterns, in which both sexes would "mother" equally, can prevent this splitting which takes place in the core stages of development. For unless men too can become objects of first attachment and ambivalence, this situation cannot change. In describing her choice of title, and her theme, Dorothy Dinnerstein writes:

> Myth-images of half-human beasts like the mermaid and the minotaur express an old, fundamental, very slowly clarifying communal insight: that our species' nature is internally inconsistent; that our continuities with, and our differences from, the earth's other animals are mysterious and profound; and that in these continuities, and these differences, lie both our sense of strangeness on earth and the possible key to a way of feeling at home here.

She speaks of the fact that "by 'human malaise' [she means]

> our species' normal psychopathology, which has pervaded our cultural—and perhaps even the more recent stages of our physical—evolution: the maladaptive stance, chronically uncomfortable and at this point critically life-threatening, that humanity maintains toward itself and toward nature.

She writes:

> What I shall *not* try to show here is (a) that the prevailing mode of psychological interdependence between the sexes does in fact need to be changed, or (b) that there is in fact some basic pathology shaping our species' stance toward itself and nature, a pathology whose chances of killing us off quite soon, if we cannot manage to outgrow it first, are very good indeed. *This book starts with the assumption that the reader is already wholly convinced on both these points.*

And she warns us that:

> until we grow strong enough to renounce the perni-
> cious prevailing forms of collaboration between the
> sexes, both man and woman will remain semi-
> human, monstrous.

What Dorothy Dinnerstein asks of us is a great deal, both in the way of dropping our comfortable compromises with atrocious situations which allow us to continue functioning on a day to day basis without too much anxiety, and a commitment to a will to change. She also asks us to accept material that cannot be proven conclusively and fosters no simple immediate solutions.

The writing of this book, she said, completely altered her relationship to those in her immediate life sphere, to her academic discipline, and to "the whole concept of world making" as she had previously perceived it. She had begun as an experimental psychologist, doing "comfortable, neat experiments" that could be proven right and easily accepted by the world. But a growing concern with her own actual collaboration in the "deathly overall direction" affairs on the planet have been taking, caused her to desire to examine how and why we all collaborate.

She addresses us all as equals in the need to care and enter quite deep waters which may well be far above our heads when she writes in her preface:

> We must try to understand what is threatening to
> kill us off as fully and as clearly as we can. . . . [I]t is
> a matter that we cannot help being interested in . . .
> [for] to fight what seems about to destroy everything
> earthly you love—to fight it not passively and autis-
> tically, with denial: and not unrealistically, with
> blind force; but intelligently, armed with your cen-

tral resource, which is passionate curiosity—is for
me the the human way to live until you die. . . .

To the extent that it succeeds in communicating
its point at all, this book will necessarily enrage the
reader. What it says is emotionally threatening.
(Part of why it has taken me so long to finish it is
that I am threatened by it myself.) And what the
reader must be warned against, therefore, is a temp-
tation: . . . to fasten upon the gaps in my
exposition—to welcome the presence of omissions
and oversimplifications—as a means of avoiding the
acute discomfort that must be faced if the main point
I am making is valid.

This warning, I feel, is crucial to our letting in not only
Dorothy Dinnerstein's ideas about how our current gender
roles are leading us into destruction, but all new ground-
breaking theory that assaults whatever patterns of adjustment we have grown accustomed to. Dorothy Dinnerstein
explained to me that her relationship to her academic discipline was shaken by her writing what for her field was "an
unscientific book." She had assaulted her own mode of adjustment and was creating similar discomforts in her readers.
She had deliberately chosen not to armor her work with an
overwhelming "wall of scholarly references and counter-
considerations." Yet her book had an enormous impact upon
people in a wide variety of fields seeking to find creative
ways to look at the forces which we have thought to be
beyond change in our society. What would happen if more
people would dare to enter with their total intellects the
areas of our communal life they care about?

While I was talking with Dorothy Dinnerstein, I flashed
upon an incident which had occurred in a creative writing
class when I was young and starting out. A student had just
finished reading an embarrassingly melodramatic inter-

change between two characters. Another student ventured helpfully, "He should not try to work with such large themes when he is only just beginning." "Shakespeare did," the teacher had retorted, starting to get angry. "But he is not Shakespeare," was the obvious reply. At that the teacher became absolutely violent and began to scream. "How do you know? What possibly gives you the right to say that? For all any of us know, he may be far greater than Shakespeare!" I will never forget that incident, nor will I ever rest at ease knowing that people desiring to deal with cosmic questions and ideas are being kept quiet because they may not yet be able to display much armor.

Dorothy Dinnerstein's decision to use her own well-woven thinking through of issues rather than the data with which most scholars inundate and blind us to "satisfy the readers that they are indeed conscientious toilers," was a conscious and courageous choice. She described the ponderous volumes scholars are expected to produce primarily as "threat gestures, not actual expressions of intellectual invulnerability, but gestures of being formidable and defended." This is a sad commentary on the state of intellectual pioneering.

In Dorothy Dinnerstein's case, the sense of urgency to turn the tide of world destruction far overshadowed her fears of putting her own personal infallibility "on the line." There was absolutely no question of waiting a year or two, or several decades (as Darwin did), until her theories were perfected. She did not feel it was entirely fair of me to use her case as an example and was quite quick to point out to me that there had not been the same sense of urgency behind the discovery that the world might be round, or of the unconscious, or of the fact that we might be evolved from higher apes. Still, it seemed that the need to amass sufficiently terrifying data and the need to present finished, perfected theories had perhaps kept many thinkers from realizing their fullest potentials.

If we could all become a little less concerned with being inviolable and stronger than all of the others who might possibly surpass us if allowed, we might be able to eliminate the greated portion of the busywork of amassing laboriously defended data which solidifies stances and clouds the freer forward thrust of thought. If we could let go of the threat of theft and competition, rampant where ideas are in the early stages of formation, and the feeling that ideas are finite and, once stolen, cannot grow again, ideas could be freed to become the common human property that they must be.

Over and over, we see scientists and scholars publishing and working, not according to their own rhythms or the rhythms dictated by their evolving ideas, but by the fear of theft. We see them weighing when to make their information public by the odd balancing of the mandate to establish ownership as soon as possible and the desire to be so perfect no one else later can punch holes in the theory espoused.

Meanwhile we have a situation in which the major scholars in a given field, instead of joining in the excited and mutually cross-fertilizing sharing that ought to be possible, stand on their separate pedestals and fire darts of doubts on one another's weaknesses of factual barricade. We have a situation where, over and over, the two or three important pioneers in any given field create such a public stir over their differences that the impact of their joined pioneering work can barely reach the people on the outside who might be most affected by it. And we as audience, as consumers of those journals of thought that cover the most compelling debates, learn to relish the details of the intellectual fights more than the underlying changes being hammered out.

Perhaps also the fear of theft and paranoia among those doing important work and the fear of the work itself are so enormous because the hazards and sacrifice become so total. Howard Gruber begins his book on Darwin's intellectual evolution, *Darwin on Man,* with the following dream fragment from a notebook Darwin kept in 1838:

> Sept. 21st. Was witty in a dream in a confused manner. Thought that a person was hung and came to life, and then made many jokes about not having run away and having faced death like a hero, and then I had some confused idea of showing scar behind (instead of front) (having changed hanging into head cut off) as a kind of wit showing he had honorable wounds, all this was kind of wit.—I changed I believe from hanging to head cut off (there was a feeling of banter and joking) because the whole train of Dr. Monro experiment about hanging came before me showing impossibility of person recovering from hanging on account of blood, but all these ideas came one after another, without ever comparing them. I neither doubted them or *believed* them.—Believing consists in the comparison of ideas connected with judgement.
>
> What is the Philosophy of Shame and Blushing?

Gruber comments:

> In this passage we catch a glimpse of man's thinking. We see the interplay of social and intellectual forces in Darwin's fear of punishment for thinking, . . . the change from hanging to decapitation, and the meaning Darwin ascribes to it, the dreamer's wish for immortality; perhaps Darwin would have been satisfied to know that the ideas for which the dreamer was executed would endure a century and more. . . . As in the dream, thinking is not a straightforward advance. From the thinker's own point of view, there are doubts, retreats, detours, and impasses; there are also impulsive mo-

ments of decision, leaps into the dark from points of no return. . . . The reader may be disappointed if he approaches the subject expecting a tale leading up to one climactic moment of great insight, like the dubious stories of Archimedes' bath and Newton's apple.

Darwin, Freud, almost all of our most important scientists and thinkers, unearthed patterns in the nature of the universe which activate some of our deepest, most instinctual fears. Knowing the cruelty of some of the forces in evolution, it is harder than ever sometimes to fight against what Charlotte Wolff defines as *What Is* in order to make new ways of survival that challenge the dominance by strength we so often fall back upon. Knowing how deeply scarred we are by early infancy and by unconscious patterns that we cannot wish away, it is harder than ever to work fruitfully towards real self-realization. And yet we would never again want to be without that knowledge and that challenge to surpass our age-old limitations. We would not want to be robbed of the chance to find better solutions each new insight complicating our problems has allowed. And yet we rail against and often ostracize those who first force us to take off our blinders.

I feel there is a real relationship between the courage to delve deep into the source of our despair and faith in human change. Dorothy Dinnerstein, while unveiling more and more disturbing "truth" in *The Mermaid and the Minotaur,* simultaneously frees us from the bonds of the "natural" patterns she is revealing by stating that we are "self-creating creatures" and "by nature unnatural." She assures us that "as the presence of this contradiction comes into steady focus, it becomes clearer and clearer that an obstacle rooted in what we think of as human nature cannot . . . be regarded as immutable. In this way we come step by step to face a fearful truth: that the quintessential feature of human life, along with its pervasive inner instability and stress, is its self-creating nature: its control—for better or for worse—over the direction in which it develops."

Thus her seeming pessimism becomes, when we think of it, the only realistic optimism. We talked a great deal the morning I visited her about how one needed hope and a deep love of life, to dig as far as one had to into "depressing subjects." Writing her new book, which deals with "why people can't bear to think about what they have to think about in order to preserve life on the planet," has been a deeply disturbing experience for her. While her first book was disruptive in her own mode of adjustment in both her intimate life and her relationship to her discipline (and similarly has that effect upon readers), this one tampers with a whole cosmology. In forcing her friends and students to "talk more than usual about the imminence of unthinkable events and the slim possibility that we might be able to forestall them," she threatens their whole mode of being, forcing a radically deepened self-reflectiveness and taking of responsibility. By tampering with their "livable euphoric level," she finds that she has aroused a great deal of ambivalence. Her students are hating her and loving her much more intensely recently, she says. And, all in all, it is quite hard.

When I asked Dorothy Dinnerstein, why her?, why did she feel she had to be the one to enter this so-difficult terrain?, she was hard-pressed to answer. We agreed that a deep conservatism usually seems to go hand in hand with the desire to move into threatening places. Her love for our planet is enormous and she felt that in exploring change the way she did, she was doing the only thing that she could do, given her particular gifts, not to lose everything she cares about. She could not explain why she felt driven to explore new vistas in the disturbing way she did while others sat there trying to ignore the possibility of the impending danger. But, as we sat in the early afternoon sunlight, she did tell me this story. She said:

All morning, as we have been talking, I have flashed upon this scene from early childhood. I must have been only about fourteen months old at the time. I remember I could barely walk. I wandered off to play with older children. We were in the Sheep Meadow of Central Park. My mother thought I was still playing with them, but really they were playing with a "Mama doll" about my size. So, while she thought I was safe, I took a walk. Before she realized what was going on and found me, I had crossed several streets. I remember first walking through beautiful warm golden grass, then onto a street full of people and things, without any anxiety—wandering, moving, exploring alone—not knowing what would happen next, but being interested.

This story, I think, says it all. And somehow as adults who care about the wonders of our world, we must find ways to recreate those early infant walks without anxiety and spaces for us all to ask those primal philosophic questions only tiny children dare to ask.

Acknowledgment is made for permission to reprint the following material:

International Creative Management, Inc. for the Estate of William Goyen for permission to reprint passages from *The Collected Stories of William Goyen* and *Come the Restorer* by William Goyen.

Delacorte Press/Seymour Lawrence for material excerpted from *Silences* by Tillie Olsen. Copyright © 1965, 1972, 1978 by Tillie Olsen. Also for material excerpted from the book *Yonnondio: From the Thirties* by Tillie Olsen. Copyright © 1974 by Tillie Olsen.

Tillie Olsen for permission to reprint material from the poem, "I Want You Women Up North to Know," originally printed in *Daily Worker;* "The Strike," originally printed in *Partisan Review* 1934.

West End Press, Minneapolis, MN for material from *Fudge* by Meridel Le Sueur.

George Allen & Unwin, London, for permission to reprint material from the poems of Kathleen Raine.

Enitharmon Press, London for permission to reprint material from the journals of David Gascoyne.

Oxford University Press, Oxford, England for poems from David Gascoyne's *Collected Poems* copyright © Oxford University Press 1965.

Quartet Books Inc. for material from *Bisexuality* and *Hindsight* by Charlotte Wolff.

Yale University Press for selections from *Beginning With O* by Olga Broumas.

Book Forum for reprinting the chapters which originally appeared in *Book Forum:*

"A Plea for Impassioned Reviewing" and "Djuna Barnes and 'Nightwood' " *Book Forum,* Volume II, No. 4, 1976. Copyright © 1976 by The Hudson River Press.

"Come a Spiritual Healer: A Profile of William Goyen" and "The Meeting of Two Revolutionaries" *Book Forum,* Volume II, No. 1, 1977, special issue on books and the South. Copyright © 1977 by The Hudson River Press.

"A Reminiscence with Marguerite Young" *Book Forum,* Volume III, No. 4, 1977, special issue on the literary life. Copyright © 1977 by The Hudson River Press.

"Portrait of Charlotte Wolff" and "Rediscovering Mary Webb," *Book Forum,* Volume IV, No. 2, 1978. Copyright © 1978 by The Hudson River Press. Part of this new version of "Rediscovering Mary Webb" includes material written specifically for *Precious Bane* (University of Notre Dame Press). The original *Book Forum* version of "Rediscovering Mary Webb" appeared in a slightly different form in an introduction to *Gone to Earth* (London: Virago).

"The Silent Poet: A Profile of David Gascoyne" *Book Forum,* Volume IV, No. 4, 1979. Copyright © 1979 by The Hudson River Press.

"A Plea for Intellectual Risk-Taking" *Book Forum,* Volume V, No. 1, 1979, special issue on knowledge. Copyright © 1979 by The Hudson River Press.

"Portrait of Kathleen Raine" *Book Forum,* Volume V, No. 4, 1981. Copyright © 1981 by The Hudson River Press.

"Writing and Surviving: A Portrait of Meridel Le Sueur" *Book Forum,* Volume VI, No. 1, 1982. Copyright © 1982 by The Hudson River Press.

"Coming of Age in the Thirties: A Portrait of Tillie Olsen" *Book Forum,* Volume VI, No. 2, 1982. Copyright © 1981 by The Hudson River Press.

"Unless Soul Clap Its Hands" is from "Sailing to Byzantium" by W. B. Yeats.

For the photograph of Marguerite Young, acknowledgment is extended to Tom Duncan.

For the photograph of William Goyen, acknowledgment is extended to J. Gary Dontzig.

For the photograph of Tillie Olsen, acknowledgment is extended to Leonda F. Finke.

For the photograph of Meridel Le Sueur, acknowledgment is extended to Meridel Le Sueur.

For the photograph of Kathleen Raine, acknowledgment is extended to Tara Heinemann.

For the photograph of David Gascoyne, acknowledgment is extended to David Gascoyne. Photograph by Sophie Bassouls.

For the photograph of Charlotte Wolff, acknowledgment is extended to Charlotte Wolff. Photograph by Man Ray.

For the photograph of Olga Broumas and Stanley Kunitz, acknowledgment is extended to David Holbrook.